McGRAW-HILL PROBLEMS SERIES IN GEOGRAPHY
Geographic Approaches to Current Problems:
the city, the environment, and regional development

Edward J. Taaffe, Series Editor

Wilfrid Bach
AIR POLLUTION

Richard L. Morrill and Ernest H. Wohlenberg
THE GEOGRAPHY OF POVERTY in the United States

Harold M. Rose
THE BLACK GHETTO: A Spatial Behavioral Perspective

THE BLACK GHETTO

A SPATIAL BEHAVIORAL PERSPECTIVE

HAROLD M. ROSE

Professor of Geography
and Urban Affairs
University of Wisconsin-Milwaukee

McGRAW-HILL BOOK COMPANY

New York   St. Louis   San Francisco   Düsseldorf   Johannesburg
Kuala Lumpur   London   Mexico   Montreal   New Delhi   Panama
Rio de Janiero   Singapore   Sydney   Toronto

07-053613-9

Library of Congress Catalog Card Number 70-179713
   34567890 **MAMM** 798765432

This book was set in Baskerville by John T. Westlake Publishing
Services, and printed and bound by The Maple Press Company.
The designer was John T. Westlake Publishing Services. The
editor was Janis Yates. Ted Agrillo supervised production.

Cover Photograph Courtesy *THE DETROIT NEWS*

To my son Gregory

CONTENTS

EDITOR'S INTRODUCTION

Harold Rose has written a book on the black ghetto at a peculiarly difficult and crucial time in the evolution of race relations in the United States. As future readers look back at this time of great ferment, the author and the editor can only speculate as to how the many ideas, conflicts, and proposed solutions presented in this brief volume will be viewed. Professor Rose has done an admirable job of distilling the literature so that the student of the future will have an opportunity to look back and capture some of the contentious and experimental spirit of the times. It is a recent literature, and in many instances an angry one, reflecting society's bitter harvest of years of oppression, restriction, and, at best, neglect. Although it is neither possible nor desirable to avoid value judgments, Professor Rose uses something of a dialectic technique, and in the case of many controversial questions, presents a careful exposition of opposing arguments.

As geography, *The Black Ghetto* partakes not only of the spatial tradition, but of an older, essentially regional, tradition. The ghetto is a place, and it is treated as such, with overtones of the classical regional holism that calls for treatment of social, economic, political, and other phenomena, and the interrelations between them. These interrelations are clearly functional, and the student should be able to see the ties between political and educational systems, between economic problems, cultural systems, and housing patterns. Discussion of these interrelated systems reveals a multitude of hidden penalties associated with life in the black ghetto. It is difficult to escape proximity to noxious facilities or to follow conventional, white, middle-income escape paths to the suburbs; the ties to declining inner-city employment are becoming increasingly disadvantageous; severe health and educational penalties are associated with overcrowded, understaffed facilities; the political power gap between suburb and inner city is widening; and there are frequent clashes between the values of the different components of the ghetto subsystems—young-old, Southern-Northern—as well as between the ghetto subsystem itself and other metropolitan subsystems.

In the early 1970s black and white alike stand perplexed before these problems. What are the solutions? Is it to be community control with its weak financial base, or programs operated by distant Federal or other governmental agencies? Is it to be more ghetto jobs or more dispersal to growing suburban employment centers? Is it to be a political power base consolidated around a declining inner city, or a more equitable share in a metropolitan control system? We do not really know, and the final answers will not be found in this short volume. We do hope, however, that the summaries of the ideas, the controversies, and the literature here presented will bring about a keener appreciation of the problems of the black ghetto, and will stimulate renewed and more realistic efforts to find workable solutions.

EDWARD J. TAAFFE

PREFACE

Countless words have been written about America's black communities from a wide variety of disciplinarian and philosophic perspectives. That the voice and perspective of the geographer is missing from that group comes as no surprise. One of the aims of this small volume is to demonstrate that the perspective of the geographer can lead to an enhanced understanding of the evaluation and development of urban black communities, which now serve as the place of residence of the vast majority of the nation's black population.

One hopes that this book will demonstrate the validity of the geographic perspective to students and also to professional colleagues who have chosen to shy away from it. In the case of the former, the strengths and weaknesses of the book itself will be used as bases for judging the contribution that geography might make to an understanding of the ghetto phenomenon. In the case of the latter, it simply represents a choice of what might be deemed an appropriate phenomenon for geographic investigation. But in either case it is hoped that this volume will be viewed positively by members of both groups and will lead to a greater understanding of the complexities of the problems facing black Americans from the perspective of place.

In no way can such a work serve as anything other than an adjunct to the wide variety of other materials available which focus upon a common phenomenon. But nevertheless it is an adjunct which is felt to be instructive and should serve to complement the aspatial approach to the subject which is at this time more highly developed. This pioneer effort might simply be thought of as a prologue to the geography of urban black communities, with the emergence of more definitive works to follow, as younger scholars develop the willingness and enthusiasm to devote the necessary effort to the production of treatises of greater breadth and depth than this introductory effort.

The materials presented in this book reflect both the nature of the training and the experience of the author. The limitations and rewards of both show themselves, as our former experiences are manifested in our outlook and obviously permeate our *unbiased* contributions to knowledge. The author was reared in the rural farm and small-town South and has lived in a variety of urban environments before finally becoming a resident of the urban North; the imagery of these environments is still legible, and their impact upon the human condition has been brought into sharper focus. No doubt at times there has been a blurring of images which might account for weaknesses in the book itself. It is certainly possible that many attributes of this book might be variously viewed by segments of its readership as reflecting the strengths and weaknesses of the writer's experiences in moving through this variety of environments.

Many persons have been directly and indirectly involved in the creation of this volume. To them I owe many thanks for the assistance provided. I particularly wish to acknowledge the encouragement provided by significant persons at critical junctures during my academic experience. The following persons in some way assured me that I should pursue the next higher educational goal and to them I owe much: The late Mr. Cain L. Lee and Mrs. Eileen V. Fleming, Clarke Training School, Mt. Pleasant, Tennessee; Miss Mazie O. Tyson and Miss Lois McDougald, Tennessee A & I State College, Nashville, Tennessee; the late Professor Alfred J. Wright, The Ohio State University, Columbus, Ohio, and Professor Guy-Harold Smith, also of The Ohio State University; and Mr. John W. Riley, Florida A & M University, Tallahassee, Florida. Likewise, I wish to thank Mrs. Maribee Erikson for the assistance that she provided in manuscript preparation which far exceeds that normally expected of departmental clerical staff. A word of thanks should also go to other members of the clerical staff of the Department of Geography who gave unstintingly of their time, along with Miss Linda Lutes, who has served as my research assistant during the last four years. And finally, let me extend thanks to family and friends who provided encouragement and critically responded to segments of the manuscript at various stages of development.

HAROLD M. ROSE

CHAPTER 1

BLACK URBAN DEVELOPMENT A TERRITORIAL VIEW

A resurgence of academic interest in black America characterized the decade of the sixties. Such interest was partially motivated by the momentum associated with civil rights activity, the increased visibility of black Americans as a result of their growing concentration in the nation's central cities, and the enhanced status of the social sciences within the university setting. These along with other forces spurred a trend which continues unabated as is evidenced by the continuous flow onto the market of books which have as their basis the exploration of some facet of the individual, group, or situational aspect of black Americans or black America. This trend, which was largely initiated by the sociologist, historian, political scientist, and social psychologist, has begun to pick up contributions from the other social sciences which previously devoted only limited attention to such topics.

New and rising interest in black America has been legitimated by the fact that almost all social science disciplines have begun to demonstrate some interest in aspects of urban development and/or urban problems and therefore could hardly ignore the presence of the largest group of the most recent arrivals to urban America. Even those disciplines which have traditionally devoted the bulk of their interest to primitive peoples and exotic places, anthropology and geography, have begun to turn some of their interest in this direction. It is from the perspective of the latter discipline that this book chooses to cast its lot. The territorial perspective should add to an understanding of the social processes which strongly influence the life chances of black Americans and at the same time should lend insight into the development of strategies designed to alter these life chances.

GEOGRAPHY AND BLACK AMERICA

It now appears that geography, as a social science discipline, is poised to take its place among the social sciences which have a more lengthy history of involvement with topics of immediate social import. This means a redirection of emphasis from the strictly physical and economic aspects of area, to that of focusing attention on the role of social variables within a spatial context. By minimizing the latter it has frequently been viewed as the unexplained variance in spatial analysis. A few of the early efforts in this area showed signs of amateurism and were long on geography but weak on an understanding of black America. There are signs that this stage of development is almost complete, as recent contributions to the literature on geography and black America demonstrate. The nature of geographic research will strongly influence the manner in which problems of black America are handled. In that respect the geographer will be expected to make his contribution in a way similar to that in which anthropologists have adapted their standard operating procedures to permit them to turn their attention to a previously overlooked area.[1] Geography, as a discipline, seems peculiarly suited to make contributions at what Lerner had identified, in his discussion of "The Negro American and His City," as the point of convergence of person, place, and culture.[2]

There is growing evidence that a number of younger scholars embarking upon careers as professional geographers are beginning to show interest in research problems which bear upon the future of black America. Admittedly, interest of this sort might simply represent where we are in the process of social development today, as opposed to a generation ago. The following example indicates where we were only slightly more than a generation ago. In 1938 A. E. Parkins in his classic geographic treatment of the South included only a single item in his index under the heading "Negro." The index item noted was listed "Negro Fitted to Southern Climate." The statement associated with this heading reads as follows:[3]

[1] Ulf Hammerz, *Southside, An Inquiry into Ghetto Culture,* Columbia University Press, New York, 1969; Lee Rainwater, *Behind Ghetto Walls,* Aldine Publishing Co., Chicago, 1971; and Elliot Liebow, *Tally's Corner,* Little, Brown, and Company, New York 1967.

[2] Max Lerner, "The Negro American and His City," *Daedalus,* Fall, 1968, p. 1397.

[3] Almon E. Parkins, *The South, Its Economic-Geographic Development,* John Wiley & Sons, Inc., New York, 1938, p. 227.

The tropical-bred Negro, immune to the diseases of wet, hot climates, was a godsend to Southern rice growers on the low, swampy, outer margins of the coastal plain. The climate was so "deadly" there that all whites who could get away sought the mountains or the sea islands during the summer months.

In the 1970s one would expect that any general textbook treatment of the geography of the United States, and the South in particular, would hardly choose to devote so little attention to the black population.

Geography as a social science discipline has an opportunity to employ the perspective to which it has devoted much energy in developing, the spatial one, to add to the general body of social knowledge and to aid in understanding black America. Subsequently one would hope that the knowledge acquired would aid in alleviating some of the problems confronting that segment of the nation's population. One is somewhat dismayed to find that cultural geography, one of the principal divisions of the discipline, has been as guilty as other aspects of the discipline in choosing to ignore black America. The latter, though, is no doubt partially explained by the cultural geographer's obsession with artifacts of the landscape instead of culture as expressed by behavior. This basic predilection has given anthropologists an opportunity to adapt their techniques of cultural analysis to the urban environment and thus to begin to pursue topics dealing with black culture.* Cultural geography, rigidly defined, has yet to make a contribution in this challenging, but often threatening area.

THE SCOPE OF THE BOOK

The five chapters which follow are all devoted to a single aspect of black America: the evolving status of urban black populations viewed from a territorial perspective. That territory is an important element governing the behavior of Western man or, for that matter, universal man is undisputed. But the territorial perspective has been given short shrift in evaluating the status and problems confronting an ever increasing segment of the nation's black population. The limited attention given this perspective can be partially attributed to the orientation of the disciplines which have devoted attention to the problem and, no doubt secondarily, to the fact that territory is

*While there is increasing evidence of relevant works of an anthropological nature designed to shed light on the culture of urban black populations, a number of classic works were prepared by black scholars during an era in which such topics were given only minimum attention.

generally viewed as economic land or property over which blacks in America have had little control.

Since most urban black populations are spatially concentrated in one or more contiguous areas in the nation's principal population centers, the central focus of this book is on place. Place in this instance is identified as the "black ghetto." The choice of the identifying nomenclature is tentative and simply expresses the status attributed to most black Americans and subsequently to their places of residence in urban centers. The use of terminology of this sort was questioned recently. Increasing concern has been expressed regarding its adequacy or appropriateness by both black and white scholars, as well as by the residents of the area of occupancy. The continued use of the term "ghetto" in this instance reflects the author's view of the seemingly unchanging process which operates to allocate housing to black people. To date, the housing allocation mechanism operates under conditions which lead to black residential concentration and spatial segregation. Until blacks have free access to residential locations within their economic means, the ghettoization process can be said to be operative. Then and only then will the ghetto designation have lost its validity.

Because the term has often been employed as a synonym for the term "slum," many middle-income blacks, in particular, are offended when the term is applied to areas in which they reside. But Drake has said that such areas are simply "gilded ghettos" and that the character of black residential areas are not set by them.[4] The position taken by Rasmussen finds the term "ghetto" to be too imprecise and one which leads to confusion. More specifically, he has said the following in criticizing the use of this terminology:[5]

> Ghetto is no longer a satisfactory word; it has taken on such peripheral meanings as to be relatively useless to the social scientist. The students and academicians now using the term not only risk being misunderstood; they may be translating confusing impressions into assumptions. In this era of social consciousness, it would seem both appropriate and necessary to clarify terms, particularly when they are judgmental.

To his, numerous other voices have been added, and one of the more recent is that of Murray, who is unduly critical of social scientists, whose views he holds in low esteem.[6] Murray is of the

[4] St. Clair Drake, "The Social and Economic Status of the Negro in the United States," *Daedalus*, Fall, 1965, p. 777.

[5] Karl R. Rasmussen, "The Multi-ordered Urban Area: A Ghetto," *Phylon*, Fall, 1968, p. 282.

[6] Albert Murray, *The Omni-Americans*, Outerbridge and Dienstfrey, New York, 1970, p. 25.

opinion that social scientists offer very little in the way of meaning-ful analysis of black America through their survey research efforts. Much of this work he avers is insulting to black people and cites as evidence the use of the term "ghetto," to describe black residential areas, as degrading.[7]

One could hardly disagree with these and other criticisms of the use of the term "ghetto" to describe urban black residential areas. But from the point of view of one who is process-oriented, it would be letting white Americans off the hook to deny that both individual behavior and institutional behavior results in confining most black Americans to residential areas from which there is little chance for escape. Black people may on occasion make successful adaptations within their circumscribed territories and choose to deny that social institutions over which they have no control determine, within broad general limits, their zone of residence. Thus, it does not appear improper to describe as ghettoization the residential allocation process which limits on other than economic grounds one's choice of place to live.

Because of the negative connotations assoicated with this termi-nology, black people may well choose to reject such externally assigned descriptions describing residential areas in which they constitute the majority population. Such a rejection is, indeed, a valid one, as a group should have the right to define itself and, subsequently, the extension of itself, its zone of residence. But until one has the power of choice in the decision to seek residential accommodations outside the territory set aside, directly or indirect-ly, for that purpose, to deny the operation of socially constraining forces is to boast of freedom while still a prisoner. Little is resolved in arguments of this sort, especially when terms used in the social science sense become problematic in everyday usage. The term "ghetto" as it is used in this book simply refers to the territory which is occupied by black people in American cities and which has evolved out of a system of residential allocation permitting no freedom of choice. In this instance the term itself does not connote quality of environment or social status, but simply refers to a residential enclave in which ultimately the only competitors for housing are members of a single race.

The Spatial Identification of the Black Ghetto

The contention here is that the black ghetto represents a social area primarily made up of persons of a single race and possessing similar subcultural characteristics. Oftentimes such simply stated definitions

[7] *Ibid.*

do not ease the geographer's task of translating the concept from an aspatial to a spatial one. In order to operationalize the definition it is necessary to establish criteria which enable one to identify areas which fall into this category. The first problem is that of selecting a territorial unit of appropriate scale which might be used as the building block for the developing ghetto. The smallest unit for which there is available data on the racial characteristics of the population is the census block.[8] Thus the racial composition of a single block, at some given point in time, can be expected to set the stage for an evolving pattern of racial dominance which will see block after block go through the process of racial change. The block, then, is considered the most appropriate unit for which there is readily available data that permits one to observe changes in racial composition within a territorial context. While the census block is a much more sensitive unit within which to observe the phenomenon of racial turnover, it is the aggregate of census tracts which more nearly conforms to the neighborhood scale. Thus, it is this series of contiguous neighborhoods which might be described as the ghetto spatial configuration. The census tract, then, is the territorial unit employed to identify ghetto neighborhoods (Figure 1.1).

The question of the appropriate population mix which justifies the use of a set of descriptive labels specifying the racial status of the population at a given date is not easily resolved. Like a number of previous writers, this writer will use the proportion of the population residing within a neighborhood at a given date to identify it as part of one social area or another. When the population within a given census tract equals or exceeds 50 percent black, then that tract will be said to constitute a ghetto neighborhood. Ghetto core neighborhoods are represented by census tracts whose population is 75 percent or more black, with ghetto fringe neighborhoods having 50 to 74 percent of their population identified as black. Variations in intensity of black occupancy is thought to be significant in actuating whites into moving, as well as attracting additional black residents. Zones contiguous to the ghetto core and fringe, if they contain a black population that constitutes 30 percent or more of the total population within their domain, are thought to represent neighborhoods in transition. Thus the ghetto is essentially made up of neighborhoods in which blacks constitute a clear majority and have generally assumed dominance over local social institutions; neighborhoods in which dominance is incipient and change continues at a rather rapid pace; and neighborhoods in which blacks do not yet

[8] Harold M. Rose, "The Origin and Pattern of Development of Urban Black Social Areas," *Journal of Geography*, Sept., 1969, p. 327.

Figure 1.1 Ghetto clusters, ghetto neighborhood types, and intensity of black occupancy at the block level. The San Francisco case, 1960.

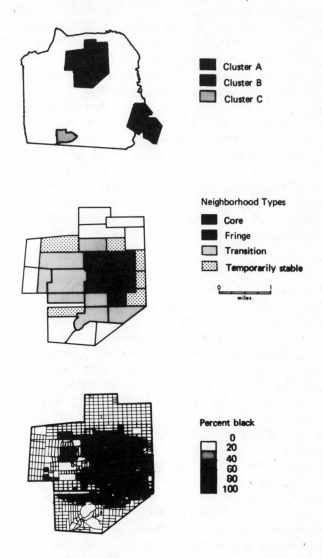

constitute the dominant population, but are found in large enough numbers to hasten the future outmovement of the white population.

The descriptive categories assigned to such neighborhoods vary from writer to writer. The Taeubers employed such categorical descriptions as "Established Negro Areas," "Zones of Invasion," "Zones of Succession" to specify the racial composition of areas at a given point in time.[9] Once again the choice of terminology employed to describe such areas has come in for criticism. Such terms as "invasion" and "succession" are sometimes perceived by blacks as offensive, and by the same token they are viewed by whites as terms which reflect an initial unwillingness to relinquish territorial dominance and a final acquiescence in response to the entry of an alien population. To those who are unfamiliar with use of these concepts in the area of plant ecology, from which they were borrowed, they take on connotations which are conflict-laden. It has been previously pointed out that the term "residential invasion" has come to represent the white residents' perception of events in the struggle for residential space, and in all likelihood the white writer's perception as well.[10] Once an area has moved through the various stages of intensifying the proportion of blacks in its population, these proportions are seldom reversed, unless the area itself is physically transformed and starts out again as a new neighborhood possessing a neutral status.

Regional Differences in the Housing Allocation Process

A series of ghetto neighborhoods constitute a full-blown ghetto. Once a given population center of 100,000 or more becomes the place of residence of 25,000 or more blacks, the bulk of whom are universally confined to ghetto neighborhoods, it is then said that such places constitute a ghetto center. Slight variations occur from place to place in the rate at which neighborhood change takes place and the number of neighborhoods which might be identified as falling into one category or another. But the major differences tend to be regional ones, with the process of black territorial development being initially distinguishable between the South and the non-South. It now appears that a convergence of the basic residential allocation process between the two regions is beginning to take place.

Traditionally, Southern cities possessed only zones previously described as ghetto cores, as almost all areas contained populations which were essentially black or white. It is true that in some Southern cities this generalization is not entirely valid, but these are exceptions rather than the rule. Frequently a physical barrier will separate black from white areas in Southern communities, thereby eliminating the zone of transition which is commonplace in non-Southern cities (Figure 1.2). But the principal reason for the

[9] Karl E. Taeuber and Alma F. Taeuber, *Negroes in Cities,* Aldine Publishing Co., Chicago, 1965, pp. 104-105.
[10] Harold M. Rose, "The Development of an Urban Subsystem: The Case of the Negro Ghetto," *Annals of the Association of American Geographers,* March, 1970, p. 4.

traditional absence of the zone of transition is the difference in the way that housing is allocated to black populations.

Figure 1.2   Regional variations in the intensity of black ghetto occupancy on a block basis. (Source: Harold M. Rose, "The Black Ghetto as a Territorial Entity," Special Publication No. 3, Department of Geography, Northwestern University, 1969, p. 47)

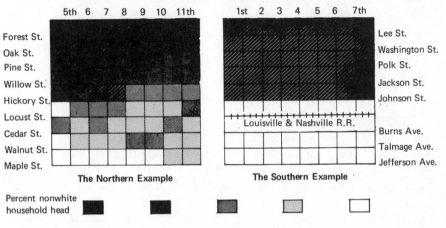

In the South a territory is allocated for the purpose of black residential development, and shelter is established within the designated zone. Outside the South blacks enter a residential zone previously occupied by whites, thereby setting white flight into motion. These basic differences have resulted in a wide variety of housing types and forms being present within black residential zones in Southern cities, whereas only those housing types located in the wake of ghetto movement have been traditionally available to blacks outside the South. Thus Southern blacks with relatively high incomes have had access to a broader range of housing types within the territory designated for black residential development than has been true of his counterpart outside the South.

BLACK CULTURE AND THE GHETTO

The ghetto presently constitutes the territorial base within which black culture is learned, transmitted, and preserved. Variant forms of black culture are evolving within the ghetto context, as many black residents must devise new ways of coping with a new and sometimes alien environment. It is fairly obvious that some scholars view aspects of forms of behavior which are nurtured by the ghetto as pathological and are inclined to attribute such behavior to human frailty. Banfield's most recent contribution, *The Unheavenly City*, is probably more outspoken on this score than anything else published by a respected contemporary scholar, although he himself denies that his is a work of social science.[11]

In assessing the nature of the urban crisis which is said to prevail in the nation's cities, an aspect of which is generally associated with the rapid postwar rise in the size of the black population, Banfield holds that the problem could essentially be eliminated given the following:[12]

> If these inner districts, which probably comprise somewhere between 10 and 20 percent of the total area classified as urban by the Census, were suddenly to disappear, along with the people who live in them, there would be no serious urban problems worth talking about.

The problems which are to be found in these areas have been attributed to the psychological outlook of a segment of its resident population. As a means of grappling with this problem, Banfield has developed a class culture schema which categorizes individuals on the basis of present and future orientedness. The problems of ghetto populations are thought to revolve around their orientation toward the present, a condition which is thought to be unchangeable.[13] It is little wonder that Murray, a humanist, seems to place so little faith in social science,[14] when social scientists of the stature of Banfield minimize the real problems faced by real people, who have adopted what many would conceive as poor strategies to deal with an environment which is not of their creation—at least, in terms of their being its architects. Few today deny the existence of a black culture or at least the existence of a modified value system which might be described as subcultural. That some of these subcultural practices create problems for their practitioners is undeniable, but it is unforgivable to create a deterministic construct which combines the notions of class and culture simply to lend credence to one's own political conviction. The rather limited scholarly contributions in the area of black ghetto culture could result in the widespread acceptance of Banfield's notions.

The contributions of a growing number of urban anthropologists might well be used to debunk some of the notions of the sort which appear in *The Unheavenly City*. Rainwater quite rightly makes the point that when a group is excluded from the normative games of the

---

[11] Edward C. Banfield, *The Unheavenly City,* Little, Brown and Company, Boston, 1970, Preface, p. 5.
[12] *Ibid.,* p. 12.
[13] *Ibid.,* p. 211.
[14] Murray, *op. cit.*

larger society it develops substitute games for itself.[15] These substitute games are learned and played out in the ghetto, for this is the one place where blacks have had the freedom to engage in expressive behavior without undue interference. The extent to which a person's life style repertoire is dominated by aspects of ghetto culture is a function of the extent to which he is barred from participation in mainstream institutions. Thus, as Drake has indicated previously, the process of ghettoization leads to the evolution of a black subculture[16] which is frequently held in contempt by the dominant society. This contempt is not confined solely to whites, but is evidenced by middle-class blacks who view practitioners of such life styles as detrimental to the welfare of the group. Tinker believes that the schism between blacks possessing a lower-class life style and those described by the term "bourgeois" works against efforts at black nationalism.[17] But increasing evidence that American society is inordinately more concerned with divisions along racial lines than along ethnic lines suggests the possibility that intragroup conflict which revolves around life style differences might be reduced.

Place and Culture

Black culture, which was nurtured in the rural South largely within that area which Lewis calls the domain of the Negro culture sphere,[18] has spread from that hearth to every major ghetto center in this country but has been modified in the process of transfer (Figure 1.3). The term "folk culture" which was used somewhat earlier to describe the behavior of what has come to be identified as black lower-class culture may no longer be appropriate. Many elements of today's life style repertoire were learned in an urban milieu and thus reflect those patterns of behavior designed to provide support in an environment that is in many ways different from that of the rural South.

Some are of the opinion that the dominant group's view of ghetto life styles acts to penalize blacks in their efforts to succeed in the larger society. The use of such terms as "disadvantaged" and similar euphemisms implies that the black experience reflects a cultural deficit that must be overcome. According to Valentine, blacks should be viewed as bicultural because they are familiar with

[15] Rainwater, op. cit., pp. 393-396.

[16] Drake, op. cit., p. 777.

[17] Irene Tinker, "Nationalism in a Plural Society: The Case of the American Negro," The Western Political Quarterly, March, 1966, p. 113.

[18] G. M. Lewis, The Distribution of the Negro in the Conterminous United States," Geography, Nov., 1969, pp. 411-416.

Figure 1.3 The hearth of American black culture and the initial set of cities with major black cultural enclaves.

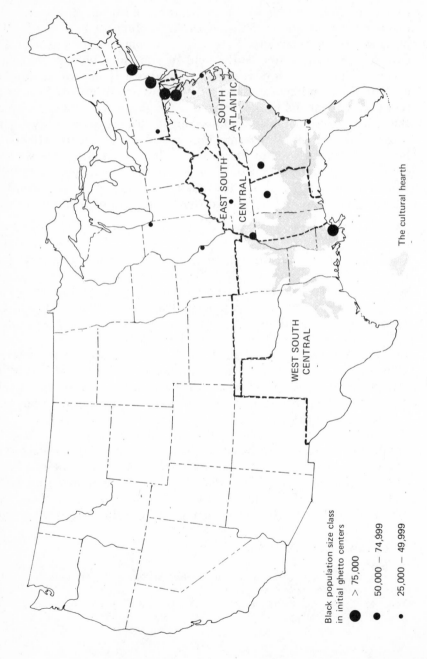

SOUTH
ATLANTIC

EAST SOUTH
CENTRAL

WEST SOUTH
CENTRAL

The cultural hearth

Black population size class
in initial ghetto centers

> 75,000

50,000 – 74,999

25,000 – 49,999

both the principal dimensions of normative culture and black culture, and it is the institutional caretakers of the dominant culture who refuse to acknowledge this situation and who tend to forever penalize segments of the black population.[19] The extent of effective biculturation, though, may be impeded by increasing isolation and conflict in cross racial interaction growing out of the selectivity of contact. Contact is increasingly limited to interaction with members of caretaker task force.

It is the principal objective of this book to review how the black ghetto as a territorial entity has shaped the life chances of black Americans through its interaction with the larger American society. And finally we will attempt to assess the future of black America as it is affected by the nature and location of the environment that serves to support the bulk of its inhabitants.

[19] Charles A. Valentine, "Deficit, Differences, and Bicultural Model of Afro-American Behavior," *Harvard Educational Review*, May, 1971, pp. 153-157.

CHAPTER 2

POPULATION GROWTH AND RESIDENTIAL DEVELOPMENT

The nation's black and other subpopulation groups identified as disadvantaged continue to grow more rapidly than the majority population. On April 1, 1970, the black population of the United States totaled 22.6 million, an increase of 3.8 million during the decade of the sixties. Blacks now constitute 11 percent of the nation's population, continuing a proportional increase which was first noticed in the census of 1940. At the time of the first census in 1790, blacks constituted 20 percent of the nation's population, but are not expected to approach that level again, at least during this century. The increasing black proportion in the total population illustrates the differential rates of growth between white and non-whites in the United States.

BLACKS AND THE DEMOGRAPHIC TRANSITION

There was a 20 percent increase in the size of the black population during the sixties, with whites showing an increase of only 12 percent. The 2 percent per annum increase in the black population places it in the moderate growth stage, requiring a doubling time of approximately 35 years. It is true that the level of growth of the black population places it at a different position in the model of demographic transition than that describing the white population, but it is also evident that blacks seem to be passing through the transition in an orderly fashion, although continuing to lag behind whites.

14

The comparison of black demographic growth patterns with those of the third world seems to be weakening. Sauvy[1] contends that population growth in all third-world countries ranges between 2 and 4 percent per annum. Since third-world countries are dominated by an agricultural economy, the increasing urbanization and the presence of a larger number of people in an urban environment for an extended period of time tend to diminish the outlines of third-world demographic characteristics. Yet there are a number of third-world countries whose annual growth rates are similar to black growth in the United States (Guinea, Mali, Mauritania, Upper Volta, Burundi, Ethiopia, Mauritius, and Nepal), but in most instances crude birth and death rates exceed those prevailing among blacks in the United States. Among third-world countries only Cuba possesses demographic characteristics that are akin to those of black Americans. Continued declines in levels of black fertility could reduce growth rates to lower levels, providing there are no significant improvements in the levels of black mortality.

During the middle sixties blacks lagged a generation behind whites in their mortality characteristics.[2] The mortality experiences of blacks have not received the same attention from demographers as has fertility, but even the latter phenomenon has only recently been the focus of scientific investigation. Sudden improvements in the mortality characteristics of blacks could depress the rate of decline in population growth, but if current trends are continued into the future, it appears that blacks will respond to the process of urbanization in a way similar to that of other groups in American society. Earlier in the decade some doubt was being expressed that urbanization might not impinge upon the fertility patterns of all groups in the same way.

BLACK POPULATION GROWTH AND THE DEVELOPMENT OF A NATIONAL GHETTO SYSTEM

Black population growth and residential development might be viewed as parts of a common package, as the former affects the demand for the latter. Thus, any treatise which focuses upon the ghetto as a spatial configuration could hardly ignore the variables of population growth and residential development and how the two interact to promote zones of residential occupancy that reflect a society's prevailing social values. In this instance one is particularly interested in changes in the magnitude and character of the black

[1] Alfred Sauvy, *General Theory of Population*, Basic Books, New York, 1969, pp. 204-205.
[2] Irene B. Taeuber, "Change and Transition in the Black Population of the United States," *Population Index*, April-June, 1968, p. 132.

population during the sixties and that population's impact on the development of a national ghetto system which has evolved during the past sixty years, but whose development has been accelerated during the post World War II period.

The present patterns of black population growth and the subsequent patterns of spatial residential development could have far-reaching implications for the United States as a nation and for black people as a social group. While these implications are not entirely clear, it is becoming increasingly evident that two spatially dichotomous populations are emerging with blacks anchored in central-city locations and whites dispersed throughout the fringing suburban ring. The hostility which is surfacing between the governments of suburbia and those of the central city in large measure illustrates the growing antagonisms and envy between the white suburban "haves" and the black central-city "have-nots."

The continued urbanization of the nation's population and the subsequent concentration of blacks within ghetto spatial configurations are likely to lead to a system of black city-states controlled and manipulated by those who occupy the high grounds of suburban residence. This latter possibility leads some to view the central city as the new urban reservation occupied by yesterday's people who simply maintain capital stock already amortized, but who generate a need for social overhead capital which is not generally available in adequate volume. Thus the residents of the reservation and the capital stock at their disposal both fail to live up to their inherent potential.

Urbanization Proceeds

The process of black urbanization which was initiated on a meaningful scale prior to World War II goes on unabated, as blacks continue to abandon rural areas for the bright lights of the cities. Mississippi's black population declined by more than 100,000 during the sixties with absolute losses in the black population also occurring in Alabama and South Carolina, and only limited growth being recorded among the black population in a number of other Southern states. These were the states that in 1960 were the place of residence of a relatively large black rural population.

Outmigration from the South continued, and almost all of the migrants were destined for urban centers in the North and West. By 1966 observers noted that there had been a significant slowdown in the volume of black outmigration from the South, but preliminary evidence now indicates the volume of migration during the first half of the decade had been heavier than it was assumed to be. Indirect evidence indicates that there was an upturn in the volume of migration during the last two years of the decade, as the total volume of net outmigration was only 17 percent smaller than it had been during the fifties. Continued urbanization is resulting in the decimation of the black population in the rural South, and even those larger urban places located beyond the principal Southern growth zones are experiencing growth simply as a result of natural increase which is associated with relatively high levels of fertility.

In 1910 there were only 18 urban places in the nation with 25,000 or more blacks in their population, and 12 of these were located in the South (see Figure 1.3). By 1970 there were more than 70 urban places in the nation with more than 25,000 blacks; more than half of these were located outside the South. Urban centers with black populations of 25,000 or more during some initial time period have served as the takeoff level for rapid development of expansive black residential enclaves, which have come to be identified as ghettos. Since a ghetto is generally viewed as an urban spatial configuration whose development is a principal component of emerging metropolitan systems, ghetto centers are identified as urban places with a minimum of 100,000 people, in which there are at least 25,000 black residents. By definition there are some communities whose black population transcends the critical minimum, but whose total population has not yet reached 100,000. Such communities, however, would not be identified as a part of the national ghetto system because they have not evolved as a result of black urbanization.

A previous attempt was made to identify ghetto centers on the basis of the period in which blacks initially transcended the 25,000 lower population limit.[3] Old or first-generation ghetto centers were identified as those housing more than 25,000 blacks before 1920. These constituted the premajor migration growth centers, and outside the South included the nation's largest cities. New York, Chicago, Philadelphia, Pittsburgh, and Cincinnati had attracted large numbers of blacks prior to World War I. Second-generation ghetto centers included those whose black population reached the 25,000 mark during the interval 1920-1950, and third-generation centers are those that have come into existence since 1950. Third-generation centers are currently most numerous and indicate that urbanization was most rapid during and since World War II, as the black migrant headed for a greater number of places. Among the 28 third-generation ghetto centers in existence in 1970, 13 were located in the South. Technically, some of these Southern centers probably should not be identified as third-generation centers because they have long

[3] Harold M. Rose, "Social Processes in the City: Race and Urban Residential Choice," *Commission on College Geography*, Resource Paper No. 6, Washington, D.C., 1969, pp. 3-4.

maintained sizable black populations, but they themselves were not of metropolitan character prior to World War II.

Regional Variations in the Evolution of Black Residential Enclaves

Some previous criticisms have been expressed which indicate that ghetto might be an inappropriate word to describe the urban black residential configurations which evolved within the South. Zones of black residence in Southern cities were defined by custom and in some instances even by law, and therefore the process responsible for the evolution of black territorial communities was regionally specific. The process of ghettoization is generally described as that process whereby in the process of residential selection one racial or ethnic group displaces another within a prescribed zone. Ghettoization then implies an absence of an option to a choice of housing outside of the area of racial or ethnic transition for other than economic reasons. Some have chosen to use the term "colony" to describe zones of black occupancy in Southern urban areas because they have traditionally represented areas of separate development. The colonies of the urban South have their counterpart in the black quarters in the small-town South. During the past 15 years, some evidence has been displayed which indicates that a convergence of the process of black residential development is taking place; white residents in the South are beginning to respond in a fashion similar to that characterizing whites outside the South, when zones of white occupancy are threatened by black entrance. This convergence is believed to be associated with the action of the Supreme Court in striking down de jure segregation in the schools. As long as institutional sharing was not a prime concern, physical proximity of the races was not an overriding issue. More succinctly, the process of ghettoization might be described as one in which there is an increase in the number of black households and decrease in the number of white households within some prescribed zone, a process set in motion by one group's refusal to share social space with the other.

The above distinction between the operation of the housing market in Southern and non-Southern cities will not be pursued beyond this point as ghetto has now become the standard term used to describe zones of black occupancy, wherever they tend to occur in the United States. The mass media have no doubt played a major role in providing universal acceptance for this terminology, and few laymen stop to consider the underlying process which might have contributed to a particular ghetto's evolution. From this point on, ghetto will be employed to describe zones of black occupancy regardless of their location. The term as it is used in this instance does not connote a condition of residential quality, but simply the place of residence of a segment of the black population on the basis of the intensity of spatial segregation.

The term "ghetto center" has been employed to identify those cities within a national network of cities which have more than 25,000 blacks in their total population. The actual intensity of the spatial separation of the black and white population will vary from place to place, but in no instance are blacks found to be living outside of black residential enclaves in significant numbers in any of the centers identified (Figure 2.1). During the middle sixties the Taeubers demonstrated that racial residential segration was a universal phenomenon in the United States,[4] although there was some evidence of a slight reduction in the intensity of spatial segregation in some cities between 1950 and 1960. A continuation of the reduction of the intensity of segregation might have occurred during the sixties, because the proportion of black escapees might have increased as a result of improvements in economic status and the relaxation of restrictive realty practices. But these conditions were hardly enough to have any real impact on the changing magnitude of the spatial configuration that is here identified as a ghetto. The continued migration of blacks from noncentral-city locations has resulted in the continued growth of the black ghetto.

Black Suburbanization

During the sixties the national ghetto network began to spill over into a number of suburban ring communities, as evidenced by the increase in the magnitude of the black population outside central cities in a few select locations (Table 2.1). Suburbanization of the black population is thus underway, but it is occurring essentially in the same way as did residential development in the central city. Suburban ghetto clusters can now be added to the list of ghetto centers which have facilitated escape from central-city locations and which are beginning to serve as direct magnets of attraction. Farley's recent analysis of black suburbanization showed that in 1960 the noncentral-city black population was concentrated in only 10 Standard Metropolitan Areas.[5] The metropolitan areas whose ring populations are notable by their magnitude are New York, Philadelphia, Newark, Birmingham, Chicago, St. Louis, Detroit, Washington, Miami, and Pittsburgh. In 1960 no fewer than 50,000 blacks were found within the rings of these metropolitan areas. Only six of these rings continued to attract blacks in large numbers during the sixties.

[4] Karl Taeuber and Alma Taeuber, *Negroes in Cities*, Aldine Publishing Co., Chicago, 1965, pp. 31-36.

[5] Reynolds Farley, "The Changing Distribution of Negroes within Metropolitan Areas: The Emergence of Black Suburbs," *American Journal of Sociology*, Jan., 1970, p. 523.

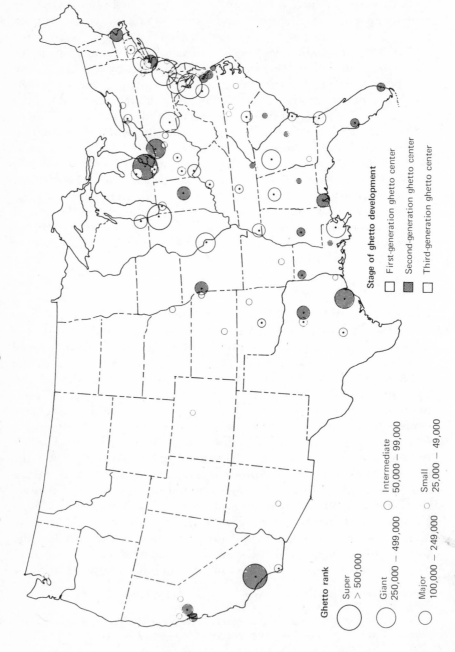

Figure 2.1   A developmental network of national ghetto centers.

Table 2.1 Major black suburban ring population centers, 1970

Place*	Population
Los Angeles-Long Beach	241,000
New York City	217,000
Philadelphia	191,000
Washington, D.C.	166,000
Newark	141,000
Chicago	126,000
Miami	114,000
San Francisco-Oakland	109,000
Detroit	97,000
Birmingham	92,000
Baltimore	70,000
Houston	66,000
Pittsburgh	65,000
New Orleans	57,000
Atlanta	56,000

*Standard Metropolitan Area
Source: *U.S. News & World Report*, March 1, 1971, p. 25.

Large-scale ghettoization of suburban populations during the sixties was essentially confined to New York, Newark, Miami, Chicago, St. Louis, and Washington, with the rate of growth in the Washington metropolitan area far outstripping the rest. Among the major black metropolitan ring communities none are associated with third-generation ghetto centers. Seven are found in the rings of first-generation ghetto centers, and three are located in the rings of second-generation centers. Third-generation centers have notably few blacks residing in their rings. Milwaukee and Denver, both third-generation centers, had only 1,000 and 3,000 blacks in their rings, respectively. It appears that this pattern is commonplace among centers at this stage of development.

The individual municipalities within the suburban rings witnessing a rapid increase in the growth of their black populations tend to represent older suburbs. Farley has demonstrated that this is especially the case in describing both New York and Chicago suburban growth patterns.[6] Thus it appears that blacks frequently serve as a replacement population for whites who are beginning to move to more affluent suburban communities. So the rapidity of black suburbanization is partially conditioned by the relative attractiveness of older suburban communities to suburbanizing whites.

The situation in Southern metropolitan areas characterized by sizable black populations in noncentral-city locations has developed

[6] *Ibid.*, pp. 517-521.

under a different set of circumstances. In many instances it is inappropriate to designate such communities suburban, as they might more appropiately be defined as satellite communities. In a number of instances blacks constitute the majority population within the suburban ring communities (Figure 2.2). The redistribution of the black population toward the suburbs carries with it some economic advantages, but the process which describes this redistribution does not differ significantly from that which operates to allocate blacks to prescribed zones within the central city.

Figure 2.2   The percentage of blacks in selected Miami suburban communities, 1970.

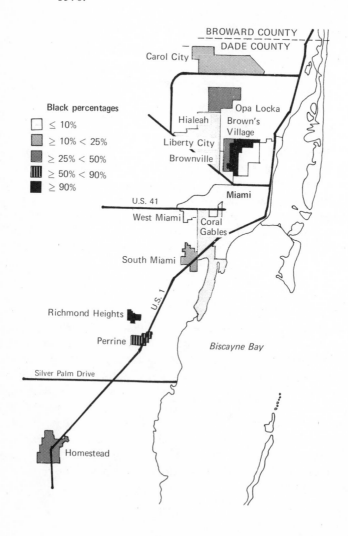

THE ROLE OF POPULATION GROWTH FACTORS

Changes in the size of the black population within the nation's central city ghettos reflect changes in the level of fertility, mortality, and net migration. These forces acting in combination serve to regulate growth rates. Black growth rates, unlike those associated with other identifiable groups in American society, are almost totally conditioned by internal change in the level of growth forces. Immigration is not a significant growth factor among urban blacks, although some writers have described black outmigration from the rural South as analogous to European immigration in terms of its impact on the development of black residential enclaves. While there are some similarities among these phenomena, black population growth has been entirely conditioned by the American environment. During the previous two decades the black experience which has conditioned ghetto growth has been the massive volume migration from rural and small-town environments to large central cities and the transfer of levels of fertility characterizing the area of origin to the areas of destination. Declining levels of mortality have aided in accelerating rapid growth under conditions of urbanization.

Black Fertility Patterns

Black fertility levels continue to remain higher than those characterizing the white population, but there is evidence which indicates that black fertility trends continue to parallel those of the white population with a time lag of little more than a decade. The results of the 1970 census show that levels of fertility have been depressed in all of the nation's major ghetto centers. Employing the child-woman ratio it is possible to compare changes in relative levels of fertility from place to place. The child-woman ratio is the number of children under age five per 1,000 women aged fifteen to forty-four in the population. The weakness of this index is that it simply registers the number of surviving children born during a five-year period, and thus is not a complete birth count. The error internalized in this index will vary from place to place as a function of the birth survival rate. In those communities where the level of infant mortality is high, the child-woman ratio loses some of its validity as a measure of levels of fertility.

In 1960 the child-woman ratio for the nation's black population was 694. Within urban areas the level generally ranged between 600 and 700 and in rural areas it often exceeded 800. The white population was characterized by a child-woman ratio of 472 during this same period. A cursory examination of the surviving black populations born between 1965 and 1970 would indicate, at least for the major ghetto centers, a level of fertility which typified that of the white population in 1960. Among 30 major ghetto centers, 18 were characterized by child-woman ratios ranging between 400 and 499, 8 exceeded the 500 level, and 4 maintained levels of fertility of less than 400. In 1950 the child-woman ratio for the urban black population was 424.[7] Thus it appears that the level of black fertility in 1970 is beginning to approach the level prevailing in 1950.

The level of fertility within third-generation ghetto centers tends generally to exceed the level in the older centers. Whether this reflects the level of fertility prevailing in the area of migrant origin or the short period of time that the population has been subject to the impact of urbanism is not quite clear at this point (Table 2.2). Among the selected centers, not a single first-generation center possessed a fertility level as high as the lowest level among the third-generation centers. The level of fertility prevailing in Chicago approached that of Denver, which was the lowest of the group of third-generation centers. The volume of black migration to Chicago and the principal source region for that migration no doubt aid in maintaining relatively high levels of fertility.

Table 2.2 A comparison of black fertility levels in selected first- and third-generation ghetto centers

First-generation centers	Level of fertility (child/woman ratio)
Atlanta	428
Chicago	460
Baltimore	446
Birmingham	427
New Orleans	445
New York City	416
Washington, D.C.	392
Third-generation centers	
Buffalo	476
Denver	467
Milwaukee	510
Omaha	523
Phoenix	576
Rochester	527
Seattle	513

Source: Compiled from Advance Report Series HC(VI), 1970 Census of Population

[7] Reynolds Farley, *Growth of the Black Population*, Markham Publishing Co., Chicago, 1970, p. 106.

The dampening of black fertility levels appears to be associated with the volume and rate of migration, the state of ghetto development during a previous time period, and the length of residence in an urban environment. If present trends continue, the rate of growth of the black population will be well below third-world levels by 1980. This revelation will tend to disappoint some groups in society, while comforting others. Blacks who see themselves as building a new nation might well think that the decline in rate of growth is a plot designed to stymie their efforts to secure power through increasing numbers. Some whites, on the other hand, will applaud this finding and view it as reducing the burden on the welfare system, or if they are more sophisticated, view it as a contribution toward improving the quality of the environment. No doubt the participants in this drama of fertility suppression are hardly concerned with the goals of either of the groups previously mentioned, but simply view this action as a more effective means of adapting to conditions prevailing in the environment in which they find themselves.

A further indication of the dampening of fertility within the ghetto environment is the reduction in the proportion of children under five years of age in the population between 1960 and 1970. In 1960, at the national level the percent of the nonwhite population under five was 14.5; for the black population it was probably slightly higher. It was commonplace for major ghetto centers to have 15 percent of their population in this age category in 1960 and for those which had been the recipients of large migrant populations to exceed this level. By 1970 it was commonplace for ghetto centers to have only 10 to 11 percent of their population in this category. In some large Southern cities characterized by large-scale outmigration the percentage was less than 9. Birmingham, Alabama, is a good case in point.

The Impact of the Ghetto on Premarital Births

It seems that at this point the critical issue is not the maintenance of high levels of fertility but the stage in the child-bearing cycle in which births occur and the conditions of those births. Increasingly, there is an expression of concern over the level of illegitimacy associated with the black community and the age at which these conceptions occur. Most of these illegitimate children are born to women between the ages of 17 and 19 and thereby affect the possibility of promoting a stable union, even though it has been demonstrated that most individuals caught in this circumstance eventually get married.

Between 1965 and 1967 the illegitimacy rate among the non-white population increased from approximately 26 percent of all births to approximately 29 percent.[8] The prevailing level of illegitimacy reflects a kind of adaptation that one must make in a ghetto environment as a means of social survival. The concern here as it is related to this phenomenon is not one of morality, but simply one of reviewing how a particular life style, conditioned by the external environment, can impose an economic burden on the participants that is often difficult to overcome. Teele and Schmidt recently reviewed this phenomenon and demonstrated that the manner in which the illegitimacy rates were derived was itself defective,[9] and that the technique permitted the differences in rates between whites and nonwhites to be exaggerated. At issue here is the necessity to minimize those life style characteristics which stymie efforts at survival by imposing a handicap that leads to increased dependency.

The recent rise in the rate of illegitimacy does indeed enhance the possibility of revolution by intensifying the level of frustration and estrangement within the black community which cannot be alleviated under the conditions of the existing system. Future revolutionaries are born out of the conditions which promote an adaptive mechanism leading to an early curtailment of young black women pursuing goals which promote successful survival.

The Mortality Experience

The life expectancy of black people in the United States has continued to increase, and one can now reasonably expect at birth to live to age sixty-five—slightly longer if female and slightly shorter if male. Improved access to medical care and a reduction in labor force participation in occupations that increase the risk of death have probably aided immeasurably in increasing life expectancy. In 1968 the crude death rate for the white population in the United States was 9.6 per 1,000; at the same time the nonwhite population registered a death rate of 9.0 per 1,000. The gap between the two groups is much wider than these two values indicate, since the nonwhite population is younger than the white population and thus would normally be expected to possess a lower crude death rate if the two populations were uniformly exposed to the same environments. The age-adjusted death rates for the two populations were 7.08 per 1,000 for whites and 10.77 per 1,000 for nonwhites.[10]

[8] *The Social and Economic Status of Negroes in the United States, 1969,* BLS Report No. 375, Current Population Reports, Series P-23, No. 29, p. 77.
[9] James E. Teele and William M. Schmidt, "Illegitimacy and Race," *The Milbank Memorial Fund Quarterly,* Vol. 48(2), April, 1970, part 2, pp. 128-131.
[10] *Monthly Vital Statistics Report,* Vol. 19, No. 12, Supplements, March 29, 1971, p. 12.

The greatest improvements in the mortality experience of black Americans has been in the area of lowering the incidence of infant mortality. Farley recently pointed out that the black infant mortality rate at the turn of the century in several American cities was in excess of 300 per 1,000,[11] but by 1967 it had been reduced to approximately 24 per 1,000. Even though the infant mortality level has been reduced more than tenfold since the beginning of the century, there is still room for improvement given the general level of development of national health care.

The fortunes of the nation's black population will continue to be conditioned by net natural increase in the population at the national level, although at the local level the role of migration might be highly significant. A continuation in the level of fertility reduction can be anticipated, and this should logically be accompanied by improvements in the incidence of mortality. A reversal of this situation might well indicate that ghetto life styles and subsequent orientations have become completely divorced from those in the larger society and that the ghetto condition has reached a level beyond which further attempts to ameliorate mortality status are highly unlikely.

Migration and the National Redistribution of the Black Population

Migration continues to serve as an important catalyst accelerating the rate and magnitude of ghetto development. The reduced volume of outmigration from the South only slightly altered the rate of ghetto development, and even then its impact was highly selective. In the East, ghetto growth continues rapidly in partial response to the large volume of outmigration from the South Atlantic Census Division, with South Carolina and North Carolina being the principal source areas. Only Pittsburgh among major Eastern ghetto centers recorded a low growth rate during the sixties, and this is merely the continuation of a pattern that was initiated during an earlier decade. In the North Central Division there is increasing evidence that some of the first- and second-generation centers either are no longer attractive to black migrants or their resident populations are being attracted to other places. St. Louis, Cleveland, and Cincinnati all suffered a net loss in population during the decade which can be attributed to migration. Neither of these locations, though, suffered an absolute loss in its black population.

Western cities continue to serve as magnets attracting black migrants, but even here the rate of change has slowed down. San Francisco, which was a major magnet of attraction during the World War II period, was the least attractive of major West Coast ghetto

11 Farley, *Growth of the Black Population,* op. cit., p. 70.

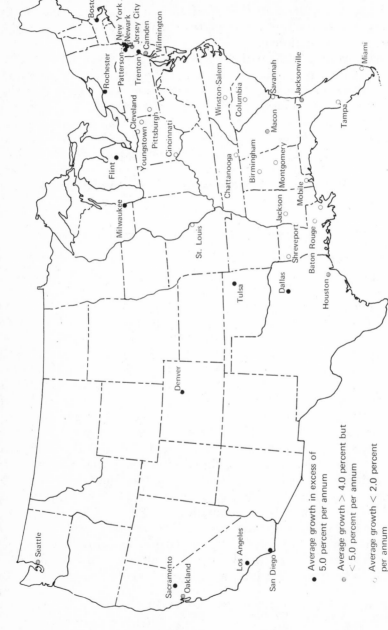

Figure 2.3 The impact of black migration on selected ghetto centers, 1960-1970.

centers during the sixties. Oakland, with a larger black population base in 1960, grew much more rapidly than its neighbor across the bay during the 10 years that have since elapsed. Growth rates in almost all centers were lowered between 1960 and 1970, but much of this can be attributed to differences in the base populations in those two years. While a relative scaling down of growth rates is apparent, growth in excess of 4 percent per annum is indicative of major migrant destinations (Figure 2.3).

Southern central-city black populations, which were slow-growing during the fifties, continued to suffer losses as a result of net outmigration. This might indicate that many migrants from the rural South who had initially stopped in Southern cities were now bypassing those centers for non-Southern destinations, or that second-generation urban populations were leaving Southern cities faster than incoming blacks from rural and small-town locations could replace them. In either case, only a few Southern cities were characterized by a rapid increase in their black populations. Unless a counterflow of migrants from non-Southern cities begin to trickle back home, Southern urban growth will be largely dependent upon natural increase. Most of the handful of growth centers in the South are located in the Southwest. Dallas and Houston continue to attract black migrants, and Tulsa has also become a migrant destination. It appears that major black urban growth in the South has coincided with total major urban growth in the South, a condition associated with the rise of new economic opportunity on an extensive scale.

Miami, with one of the most rapidly growing black communities in the South during the fifties, was relegated to a position of minor growth during the sixties. No doubt the huge influx of Cubans during the decade dampened the available opportunities for black migrants with only low-level service skills. Changes occurring within the economy of the South have not been adequate or of the nature that would make Southern cities attractive migrant destinations for a black population possessing low-level skills. The data available at this time does not allow one to make highly definitive statements about the characteristics of migrating black populations, and until this data becomes available, one can only conjecture about the characteristics of the migrating population.

The impact of differential migration on the growth of black ghetto communities is strongly brought home by reviewing the data on black population growth in several cities that possessed black populations in excess of 50,000 in 1960. Two of these cities were characterized by rapid growth, one by moderate growth, and two by slow growth (Table 2.3). Using indirect evidence, it is possible to demonstrate the combined direct and indirect effect of migration on

Table 2.3 The impact of differential migration on black population change
in a selected set of cities, 1960-1970.

City	1960 black population	1970 black population	Percent change	Estimate of change due to net migration
Boston, Mass.	63,000	104,000	65.7	+31,000
Miami, Fla.	65,000	76,000	16.7	− 2,000
Milwaukee, Wis.	62,000	105,000	68.2	+31,000
San Francisco, Cal.	74,000	96,000	29.1	+ 7,200
Shreveport, La.	56,000	62,000	09.1	− 5,200

total growth. It was previously noted that the nation's black population increased by approximately 20 percent during the decade. This implies a 2 percent per annum rate of increase. If a straight-line 20 percent increase is added onto the base population in each of the selected places, this would provide us with the 1970 population estimate, minus migration. One acknowledges the inaccuracy in these estimates owing to variations in natural increase from place to place, but it is assumed that for purposes of illustration these variations are likely to produce only minor errors.

In both Milwaukee and Boston the magnitude of the increase owing directly and indirectly to migration amounted to approximately one-half of their 1960 populations. The indirect effect of migration is reflected in the number of children produced by the migrant population once arrived at its destination. Given that the migrant population is overrepresented in those age groups in which the incidence of child-bearing is at a maximum, this could in some instances cause the indirect effect to approach the direct effect in terms of the number of persons added to the population. Boston and Milwaukee experienced similar magnitudes of population growth during the decade, but Boston posted a much greater change in the zero to four age category which no doubt indicates a higher level of growth than can be attributed to the direct impact of migration. San Francisco, with over 10,000 more blacks than Milwaukee or Boston in 1960, finished the decade with 9,000 fewer blacks than Milwaukee and 8,000 fewer than Boston. While San Francisco is still the destination of a number of migrants, it is clearly a center in which migration contributed only minimally to growth during this period.

Both Miami and Shreveport suffered a net loss due to migration. Growth was sustained in both instances only as a result of the prevalence of high levels of fertility. Paradoxically, Miami, a Southern city which led among black growth centers during the fifties, failed to attract blacks during the sixties. The Miami growth situation, though, is no doubt obscured by the fact that more than half the blacks in the metropolitan area reside in the ring, and growth of black population in the ring was on the order of increase of the faster growing, black central-city populations. Shreveport, on the other hand, continues to represent a center of net outmigration.

Migration Causation .

Some set of causal factors continues the vast outpouring of blacks from the South which started more than three decades ago. Many scholars explain this phenomenon on economic grounds. It is generally conceded that the push factor rather than the pull factor has been the principal catalyst promoting black abandonment in the rural and small-town South. Hamilton describes the situation in the following way: " . . . consequently, migration, short of living in abject poverty if not actually starving, is the only recourse for this surplus youth population."[12] This position is also supported by Persky and Kain who state:[13] " . . . that declines in agricultural employment are determined not by the pull of the cities, but rather the technological changes and market conditions that have ruled Southern agriculture crops. The jobs have disappeared before the people."

As the South has been transformed into a developed region over the last 30 years, it can no longer accommodate its home-grown and often ill-prepared black labor force and has thus dispatched it elsewhere to secure a tenuous living with the limited skills provided it in the area of origin. The South is beginning to serve as a migrant destination zone for white migrants from outside of the region who fit well into the changing economy. Inner-city ghettos, then, can attribute one aspect of their growth to the changing nature of the Southern economy.

There are those who now wish to alter the rate of black migration from Southern to non-Southern sections of the country because of the perceived social dynamite which is building up in the nation's central cities and the conflict in life styles that has accompanied the patterns of redistribution of the nation's black population. Legislation designed to enhance economic opportunity in Southern rural areas has also been implicitly concerned with slowing down the migrant flow from these areas of limited economic opportunity. Not only are governmental agencies showing interest in this phonomenon, but some black groups themselves see advantages in blacks initiating economic independence. These latter efforts have only recently surfaced and are not likely to have any far-reaching

---

12 C. Horace Hamilton, "The Negro Leaves the South," *Demography,* Vol. I, 1964, p. 278.
13 Joseph J. Persky and John F. Kain, "Migration, Employment and Race in the Deep South," *The Southern Economic Journal,* Jan., 1970, p. 275.

impact on migrant behavior. What is obvious, though, is that the volume of black migration from the South will eventually be reduced through the depletion of the ranks of the potential migrants.

Mississippi, which has generated more black outmigrants than any of the other Southern states during the past generation, is a good case in point. If it continues to lose the blacks at the recent rate and at the same time undergoes a condition of fertility decline, its migrant potential will be sorely reduced. Almost half of that state's net loss of black population was concentrated in the Delta counties, a subregion where the economic gap between its resident black and white population exceeds that of any other part of the state.[14]

There is evidence that blacks migrating from this zone during the fifties were probably more sensitive to social characteristics than to economic characteristics prevailing in the area of destination. The limited influence of the economic characteristics of place of migrant destination might have been obscured by the nature of the economic variables employed in the analysis. Kaun recently noted that black migrants from the South during the 1955-1960 period did not exhibit much sensitivity in regard to variations in the level of unemployment prevailing in a set of destinations in making their decision to move.[15] This does not imply that migrants were unaware of differing economic conditions, but that this particular variable was not significant in influencing migratory behavior. It is the social contacts with friends and relatives who have left the area that serve as a stimulus promoting continued migration into areas in defiance of the operation of economic conditions which would normally dampen enthusiasm for migration. Kaun was likewise of the opinion that the differential level of welfare payments may, in fact, be an inducement to some potential migrants to settle at a given location, a rational economic judgment, indeed, given their economic status in the area of origin. The motives prompting blacks to migrate are complex and involve economic, social, and psychological dimensions which vary in terms of their strength from individual to individual and place to place.

It was demonstrated during the previous decade that intermetropolitan migration now accounted for a larger volume of black migration than the previously detailed rural-to-urban pattern.[16] This phenomenon has not received extensive attention, but it certainly

[14] Mark Lowry II, "Race and Socio-Economic Well-Being, A Geographical Analysis of the Mississippi Case," *The Geographical Review*, Oct., 1970, pp. 516-521.

[15] David E. Kaun, "Negro Migration and Unemployment," *The Journal of Human Resources*, Vol. 2, 1970, p. 196.

[16] Karl E. Taeuber, "The Negro Population in the United States," in John B. Davis, ed., *The American Negro Reference Book*, Prentice Hall, Englewood Cliffs, N. J., 1966, p. 125.

continues to represent a major path of movement. The growth of third-generation ghetto centers probably feeds heavily upon migrants who were reared and educated in older ghetto centers. Intermetropolitan movement has altered the character of the migrant population and has created new migrant streams as well. The non-South with its large black population is now in a position to generate development of new ghetto centers without having to rely upon an influx of blacks from the cultural hearth.

THE HOUSING MARKET

Changes in the size of the black population in the nation's central cities naturally result in some necessary adjustments in the housing market. Increases in the size of the population, especially when migration accounts for a significant proportion of that increase, result in a rapid expansion of the demand for additional housing. The bulk of the housing which is made available to increasing central-city black populations is located in areas adjacent to those that have already earned the ghetto label. Thus the ghetto continues to absorb housing in its wake as a function of the demand created by changing population size.

RECENT TEMPORAL DIMENSIONS OF THE GHETTOIZATION PROCESS

Housing is allocated within this restricted market on the basis of income and life-cycle stage of development, with the better housing going to the more prosperous and the residual to those with limited purchasing power. It is too early to make definitive statements which assert that the ghetto housing market operated very much in the same way during the sixties as it had during earlier decades. One would expect that improvements in income and the passage of legislation designed to alter the way in which the housing market operates in allocating housing to blacks might have reduced the intensity of the ghettoization process. If the housing allocation patterns prevailing elsewhere in the nation during the decade operated as they did in Milwaukee, Wisconsin, then the process of ghettoization has remained essentially intact (Figure 2.4). Approximately 95 percent of Milwaukee's black population resided in a contiguous area which was predominantly black in both 1960 and 1970.

In those cities where black population growth was less rapid, the intensity of spatial segregation might have weakened as was observed

Figure 2.4   The spatial-temporal development of a ghetto. The Milwaukee case, 1950-1970.

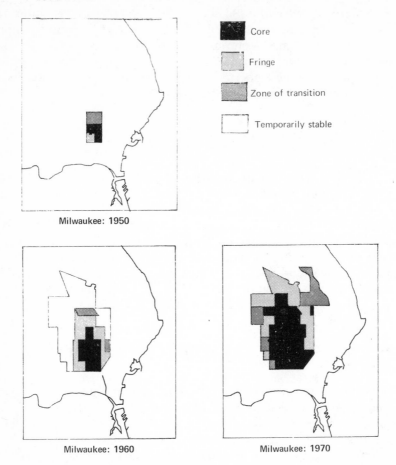

in some cities during an earlier period.[17] There is little doubt, however much the nation's population might have become enlightened, that there is still a strong aversion among whites to sharing social space with blacks. For this reason Muth contends that the real estate industry, which is a common whipping boy, should not be held responsible for the development of racially segregated residential markets, as they are only catering to the preferences of their customers.[18] The continuation of the existing process of spatially

17 Anthony H. Pascal, "The Analysis of Residential Segregation," in John P. Crecine, ed., *Financing the Metropolis*, Sage Publications, Beverly Hills, Calif., 1970, p. 403.
18 Richard Muth, *Cities and Housing*, University of Chicago Press, Chicago, 1969, pp. 106-111.

allocating housing in such a way as to promote ghetto development, even after a variety of interventionist strategies have been introduced to ameliorate the process, is causing much consternation in some circles. But the principal actors continue to behave basically the same way in the present as they have in the past, and consequently continued residential segregation is the rule.

First- and second-generation ghetto centers evolved during an era in which residential segregation was sanctioned by instrumentalities of the national government, as was reflected in the mortgage practices of Federally insured lending institutions. In 1948 the Supreme Court ruled restrictive covenants unconstitutional thereby tempering active attempts to promote ghettoization, but the action did nothing to alter the situation actively. A map showing the spatial patterns of deed restrictions limiting residential access to whites only, in almost any major city outside the South, would surely prompt one to question the legal distinctions between de jure and de facto segregation. The latter should prove especially interesting in highlighting the differences prevailing between the use of these terms as they are currently employed to distinguish between public school segregation in the North and South. It appears that legal sanctions of this sort supported the segregation of other social institutions which are currently viewed as having evolved without legal support.

In the South there were a number of direct attempts made to legally zone parts of cities for white and black occupancy, but in each instance these attempts were eventually overruled by the Supreme Court. But nevertheless, the inertia of both legal and extralegal actions of the past have spilled over into the actions of individuals and agencies, both in that set of places where those instruments were practices and into the newer ghetto centers as well. Thus, Denver's ghetto which was only slightly more than neighborhood size in 1940 was just as intensely segregated in 1960 as the Detroit ghetto which included more than 149,000 blacks in its population at the same time.

White Reaction to Black Neighborhood Entry

It is a well-known fact that black entrance into housing markets that were previously all white, but located adjacent to an area whose population is predominantly black, will elicit an accelerated leaving response on the part of the white population. Attempts to generalize about this situation through the use of the concept of a tipping mechanism have led to an uncovering of the principal dimensions of expected behavior. This understanding, though, does not permit precise analysis of expected behavior, because the role of race interacts upon a host of other environmental variables to promote a response that frequently defies precise predictability. Such factors as age of housing, tenancy characteristics, quality of schools, economic and social status of the population, stage in the life cycle, access to alternative housing, and the general condition of the local market all combine in various ways to impinge upon one's decision to move. Add to this the commonly expressed fear that property values decline when blacks enter the owner occupancy market, and the stage is set for neighborhood transition.

There is still much discussion surrounding the validity of the latter concept, and there have been few works of a definitive nature that have treated this phenomenon. Even the results of the most definitive study to date, that of Laurenti, were recently considered of questionable validity, given the manner in which the research was designed.[19] The role of race on property values and rental costs, it seems, is seriously affected by the general level of demand for housing, and by the level of black demand and the subsequent outcome of white response to the entry of blacks into previously all-white areas in terms of leaving rates.

A review of the vacancy rates in black entry zones and zones of expected entrance prevailing in 1960 in both Boston and Milwaukee reveal vacancy levels that are substantially higher than those characterizing the city at large. But even within these zones there was much variation in the vacancy level from block to block. If, under conditions of accelerated vacancy, the black demand for housing is not sufficiently high, and other whites eliminate these zones from among their list of possible choices, then one should logically expect a decline in value. It appears that value in some instances might have been upheld by the extensive demolition of housing in the core of black residential areas, thereby shifting the demand to adjacent white areas where vacancy rates are known to be rising.

Demolition activity, which in some instances constitutes an aspect of urban redevelopment, at least temporarily hastens the spatial expansion of the ghetto configuration. The manner in which cleared areas are redeveloped when demolitions are part of clearance activities will influence the continued rate of ghetto expansion. The increased demand for housing under these conditions results in opening middle-income white neighborhoods more rapidly than working and lower-income white neighborhoods. This can possibly be attributed to the greater number of options possessed by middle-income white residents and to their lower level of tolerance of black lower-class life styles. Working and lower-class whites having fewer options are thought by some to view the situation explicitly in racial

19 Pascal, op. cit., pp. 417-418.

terms rather than social-class terms and thus are known to attempt to stymie the efforts of blacks with similar incomes to gain neighborhood entry.

Depending upon the income characteristics of blacks within a specific ghetto center, a middle-income neighborhood might undergo transition from a white neighborhood to a black neighborhood during a period of a few years, or to a black working-class neighborhood if the level of black middle-class demand is not sufficiently high. In the settling-out process the neighborhood ends up a common economic class neighborhood in most instances, regardless of race. This is to say that a neighborhood which was white middle-class in some initial time period and is transformed into a black working-class neighborhood within some specified time interval will also contain a residual white working-class population in income terms. A situation of this sort can generally be described by the presence of an older white population that is beyond its stage of maximum earnings and a younger black population that has not yet reached the stage of maximum earnings. A similar situation characterizes the changing neighborhood mix at each economic class level.

Institutional Support for Black Ghettoization

From the preceding evidence it is fairly obvious that blacks continue to secure housing in racially restrictive housing markets. The strength of the role of social institutions vis-à-vis orientations of individual behavior plays an uncertain part in this continuing pattern. Whites continue to refuse to enter areas once the black proportion of the total population has exceeded their own internalized threshold of tolerance, while blacks, on the other hand, do not frequently search for housing at great distances from their place of previous residence. Thus the filling-in of zones of high vacancy on the margins of the existing black ghetto is a natural outcome of previously established behavioral patterns describing white and black behavior within a common market. But no one can deny the supportive role of social and economic institutions which, while no longer providing flagrant support for this behavior, have not completely withdrawn their implicit support.

A feeling for that support is reflected in the discussions surrounding efforts to provide housing for low-income blacks in Indianapolis, some of whom had been uprooted by public action. The following statement which was recently attributed to the mayor of Indianapolis is indicative of the situation which prevents the operation of a free housing market. "'Anyone,' said the Mayor before the Indianapolis Hebrew Congregation during the winter of 1968, 'who stands for and pursues open housing, walks a mined field. He walks dangerous ground.'" Help from the mayor would be given, conditioned on relative safety.[20]

It is apparent that any attempt to alter the way in which the housing market operates to concentrate blacks in one or more enclaves within a city is still considered a politically explosive situation. Thus the findings of Sudman, Bradburn, and Cockel, which show 19 percent of the American population to be residing in integrated areas, though only 3 percent were found in substantially integrated areas outside of the South, are understandable.[21] In this study a racially integrated area was defined as one in which both blacks and whites were entering a common housing market. It appears at this point that few persons, black or white, have had any sustained expereince in a residentially integrated environment.

Location and Black Residential Development

The initial location of the black housing market in the older areas of the city and its subsequent expansion out from this initial zone of entry severely restricts the housing types available to blacks at a given point in time. Most of the housing in the wake of the ghetto eventually becomes available to prospective black occupants provided there is no abrupt change in housing values within a short distance from zones of previous black occupancy. When housing markets with sharply differentiated price levels abut upon one another, the direction of ghetto expansion is routed around this edge and/or secondary clusters appear elsewhere to accommodate the specific needs of a segment of the black population. The availability of a variety of housing options largely depends upon the age of the city and the size of the black population.

The principal direction of ghetto development is sectoral with growth being essentially channeled along a corridor which is formed near the edge of the downtown commercial districts and through time might extend to the periphery of the city or, if given sufficient pressure, push into adjacent suburban districts. In those cities possessing super ghettos, several corridors or sectors of development are known to exist. Under the rising pressures of low-income housing demand, alternate sectors are opened to black occupancy as a means of more readily processing that demand.

[20] Daniel J. Baum, *Toward A Free Housing Market,* University of Miami Press, Coral Gables, Fla., 1971, p. 98.

[21] Seymour Sudman, Norman M. Bradburn, and Galen Cockel, "The Extent and Characteristics of Racially Integrated Housing in the United States," *The Journal of Business,* Jan., 1969, pp. 50-57.

Black residential enclaves in noncentral locations are sometimes initiated by the location of public housing sites beyond the confines of established ghetto space. Thus the increase in black occupancy in the traditional public housing developments on occasion serves as the catalyst promoting the development of a residential enclave served by the private housing sector. While it is not uncommon to detect the presence of smaller black residential enclaves within cities, to date they provide residential accommodations for only a small proportion of the total black population. Sectoral expansion remains the principal pattern of ghetto development. While axial and sectoral expansion occur simultaneously, the prevalence of a larger middle-income group at increasing distances from the core speeds expansion in that direction.

THE GHETTO HOUSING MARKET AND RESIDENTAL CONDITIONS

The restrictive nature of the ghetto housing market promotes conditions which lead to housing blight. Many young black families with low incomes have access to only the least desirable units among a supply that does not offer much in the way of options. Likewise, the intensive use of housing that is already on the threshold of deterioration shifts it from the standard category to the substandard category within a very few years, as the rate of structural deterioration begins to accelerate beyond some critical age. Given income characteristics, life-cycle stage of development, and family size, slum formation appears all but inevitable.

Inner-city ghettos are among the very few areas within a metropolitan area where the stage in the life cycle is more nearly coincident with those prevailing in the newer suburbs. Thus, the newest set of immigrants to the city are forced into the same housing units that provided shelter for previous immigrants during earlier generations when that housing stock itself was much younger. It is the black homeowner who buys on the margin of the ghetto where the housing is more attractive who finds that within a short period of time vacancy rates have gone up and housing which was previously owner-occupied is now transformed into rental units managed by commercial agencies. Maintenance goes down and so does the appearance of the neighborhood, with the result that such pioneers take a beating on their initial investment. This situation is dramatically brought home where such areas become the target for urban renewal or other developmental activity, and owners are offered only a fraction of their outstanding indebtedness on the mortgage. The redevelopment of these zones reduces the volume of substandard housing in the aggregate, but sets into motion forces which recreate a similar situation at an alternate site. As the ghetto tends to engulf that set of black movers who are engaged in noncircular moves within ghetto space, housing deterioration continues to engulf an ever larger segment of the ghetto.

The Availability of Sound Housing

In 1960, 44 percent of the nation's nonwhite population resided in substandard housing, a decrease from 72 percent in 1950.[22] At this same date only 13 percent of the nation's white population occupied substandard dwellings.[23] The substandard definition employed by Frieden was the one developed by the Bureau of Census which confines itself to a few questions concerning physical quality and the presence or absence of basic hygienic facilities. Many housing analysts contend that the census definition of substandard overlooks a number of critical dimensions and allows much housing to be defined as standard that might be classified as substandard if more vigorously appraised. The Census Bureau dropped its housing quality classification from the 1970 census enumeration form although it continued to collect information on the availability and extent of private access to basic hygienic facilities. It appears that the dropping of this question was related to the difficulty of adequately assessing physical conditions, particularly as one moved toward the extensive use of the self-enumeration technique. The move from rural to urban areas was thought to have exacerbated the slum housing situation of a sizable segment of the black population during the fifties since the worst housing in the nation was located in rural environments. During the sixties, as black urban growth was heavily directed toward the older cities of the Northeast, one can only conjecture about the extent to which housing improvements have accompanied this redistribution of population.

HOUSING PROGRAMS AND PRACTICES

The inability of a sizable segment of the black population to secure standard housing has resulted in a variety of attempts to devise programs to increase access in this area. Access to standard housing is essentially associated with a lack of adequate capital and the restricted nature of the market. For those whose incomes are so low that a disproportionate amount must be spent on housing, frequently up to 35 percent, intervention from the public sector has been necessary to increase access to standard housing.

[22] Bernard J. Frieden, "Housing and National Urban Goals: Old Policies and New Realities," James Q. Wilson, ed., *The Metropolitan Enigma,* Harvard University Press, Cambridge, Mass., 1968, p. 172.
[23] *Ibid.*

The Public Housing Program and Ghetto Development

The nation's public housing program was introduced in 1937 and has served to assist persons to satisfy their basic shelter needs during critical periods in their lives. Public housing today, while never attaining the level of units initially recommended by Congress, serves to house blacks and elderly white poor. Support for public housing has waned, as its occupancy characteristics were transformed over the years. By 1965 more than 51 percent of all public housing occupants were black.[24] Freedman points out that a tipping process operates within public housing in a manner similar to that which characterizes the private market.[25] During the sixties widespread support for public housing was basically aimed at satisfying the needs of the elderly. In 1969, 41 percent of all public housing units developed were designed specifically for the elderly and another 21 percent were mixed.[26] Housing for the elderly is said to be cheaper to build, but Taggart indicates that part of the emphasis on developing public housing for the elderly is based on the lack of neighborhood opposition.[27] So, black access to public housing is partially restricted by its limited supply and the opposition to the development of public housing outside of areas of black occupancy.

Public housing for the nonelderly has become essentially a ghetto phenomenon, associated with the movement of blacks to the North. Friedman, in addressing himself to this problem had this to say:[28]

> Many whites have resented the race, class, and habits of the Southern Negroes who moved up North. The wall of white hostility forced Negroes into ghettos. Negro public housing followed them into the ghettos. There it has remained. Site, then, has been powerfully affected by race.

Cities with large numbers of public housing units under management are generally places that have large black populations (Table 2.4). It is the black poor with their limited access to the private housing market who must depend upon this sector of the housing market to satisfy their needs. In some communities this is the only housing available to large low-income families. In most major cities the approved income limit which qualifies one for public housing

[24] Leonard Freedman, *Public Housing, The Politics of Poverty,* Holt, Rinehart and Winston, New York, 1969, p. 140.

[25] *Ibid.*

[26] Robert Taggart III, *Low-Income Housing: A Critique of Federal Aid,* The Johns Hopkins Press, Baltimore, Md., 1970, p. 31.

[27] *Ibid.,* p. 28.

[28] Lawrence M. Friedman, *Government and Slum Housing,* Rand McNally, Chicago, 1968, p. 123.

eligibility is $2,500-$4,000.[29] In 1966 it was reported that more than 42 percent of all families in public housing represented broken families with children.[30] Thus, public housing has become a refuge for those who have the least control over their lives, and this lack of control leads to other problems which transform this once envisioned temporary haven for the poor into an environment that guarantees relegation to a status of permanent poverty.

Table 2.4 Cities with large numbers of public housing units, 1967

	Number of public housing units	Number of requests for occupancy	Number of vacancies
New York City	64,700	89,200	117
Chicago	33,000	21,826	173
Philadelphia	15,700	6,631	118
Boston	11,000	6,600	571
Newark	10,900	5,195	240
Washington, D.C.	10,100	3,148	129
Los Angeles	9,300	1,496	334
Atlanta	9,000	2,065	79
Detroit	8,200	1,641	75

Source: *Building the American City,* Frederick A. Praeger, Publishers, New York, 1969, p. 112, 130.

The Pruitt-Igoe project in St. Louis, which, when it was christened in 1954, was thought to represent a public housing model that would resolve the housing problem of a segment of its poor, stands in testimony to the failure of the high-rise architectural wonders which concentrate and restrict the black poor to a limited territorial niche. Within these environments one is expected to adjust to the ways of the larger society. Chicago, like St. Louis and other cities that have been guilty of this approach to housing the poor, was recently ordered to cease and desist from these practices. In the Chicago case a formal complaint was lodged against the Chicago Housing Authority, a section of which reads as follows:[31]

> The first count of the complaint alleged that defendants had intentionally selected sites and assigned tenants to public housing units in a manner that maintained "existing patterns of urban residential segregation by race" in Chicago, thus violating plantiffs' right to the equal protection of the laws.

[29] *Building the American City,* Frederick A. Praeger, Publishers, New York, 1969, p. 132.
[30] *Ibid.,* p. 118.
[31] "Gautreaux v. Public Housing Authority: Equal Protection and Public Housing," *University of Pennsylvania Law Review,* Jan., 1970, p. 437.

As a means of overcoming some of the problems associated with practices which have become commonplace in public housing activities, management, and administration, the Gautreaux decision directed the Chicago Housing Authority to cease and desist from concentrating public housing in predominantly black neighborhoods. The courts recommended that units be developed beyond the territorial range which might readily lead to ghettoization in the near future. That ruling also addressed itself to the architectural style of the structures which are to be employed in housing low-income residents. Specifically, the court ordered that no public housing structure contain more than 120 people and that no structure exceed three stories in height which is to be used in housing children.[32]

While public housing continues to satisfy the basic shelter needs of an increasing segment of the black poor, public housing policy and management have promoted unanticipated problems that must somehow be overcome. Public housing will not be able to satisfy the housing needs of a rapidly increasing black population, and even among public housing eligibles, many will choose private slums to the public slums which eventually evolve. Public housing is still beyond the reach of that segment of the black population whose income level is below that which determines the lower limits of eligibility. Other governmental programs have been recently designed to bridge the gap existing between the public and private housing markets as currently structured.

The Problem of Housing Abandonments

In the major ghetto centers the housing crisis becomes more crucial daily. Continued demolitions in the ghetto to make way for public improvements other than housing and the construction of new units beyond the range of the ghetto housing market leave most black low-income residents little opportunity to secure decent shelter within a safe environment. Within only a few years the problem of inner-city housing abandonments has become critical in several of the nation's larger cities. It has been estimated that between 1960 and 1968, 180,000 apartments were abandoned in New York.[33] Abandonments are increasing as a function of the spread of blight and the financial inability or unwillingness of landlords to cope with the problem. Under these conditions landlords simply walk away or, in

[32] *Ibid.*, pp. 445-446.

[33] Housing and Urban Development Legislation of 1970, Hearing before the Subcommittee on Housing and Urban Affairs, Ninety-First Congress, U.S. Government Printing Office, Washington, D.C., 1970, p. 811.

some instances, permit the city to acquire such properties through tax delinquency procedures.

Abandoned buildings themselves promote a blighting influence which tends to hasten the further outmovement of persons from the neighborhood because of a rising fear of crime and declining neighborhood appearance. In most of the cities in which abandonment is a growing problem, the major share of the properties are in low-income black areas.[34] This had led to investigations of the potential for rehabilitating these structures and somehow creating livable environments which would reduce the pressure on that segment of the population that has the greatest difficulty in securing standard housing, the black poor. The problem tends to appear much more critical in those cities where much of the housing stock is characterized by multiunit developments and where the rate of owner occupancy is minimal (Figure 2.5).

Figure 2.5   Abandoned building in Boston. (Source: *Boston Herald*)

[34] Sheldon L. Schreiberg, "Abandoned Buildings: Tenant Condominiums and Community Redevelopment," *The Urban Lawyer*, Spring, 1970, p. 187.

Recent Attempts to Provide New Housing for Low-Income Families

Programs designed to bring new housing within the reach of black low-income populations are continually being promoted at the congressional level, but in translating the legislation into a workable program, barriers tend to evolve which stymie many well-intentioned efforts. The new 235 and 236 Federal Housing Legislation is a case in point. The former program was designed to promote home owner-ship among that segment of the stably employed population whose annual incomes were between $3,000-$8,000 by providing low interest, long-term loans with only a minimum downpayment. The latter program was designed to promote the development of rental units.

Most of the new housing units constructed under the provision of 235 legislation have been built outside ghetto neighborhoods, leading many to feel that blacks only benefit through the trickle-down process which is set in motion by the addition of new housing units to the total supply. Programs such as this have been employed to promote a policy of scattering low-income persons through the metropolitan systems. Opposition to this policy generally increases when it is assumed that low-income black persons might likely qualify for such housing beyond the limits of the ghetto. The greatest opposition to the scattered sites policy appears to be emanating from suburban communities which might serve as likely targets for 235 housing, given the cost of the existing housing prevailing within those communities. Blacks have probably received the greatest benefits from the rehabilitation aspect of the program, which permits a limited proportion of older units to be rehabilitated and marketed to low-income residents in the same way that the new units are marketed. The rehabilitation segment of the program is largely centered in older central-city neighborhoods.

Will the Housing Crisis Ever Disappear?

The continued urbanization of the nation's black population and its growing concentration in the major central cities of the country has produced a set of problems which are not easily overcome. The housing market continues to respond to this population in such a way that the evolution of giant ghettos is all but inevitable. It appears that the private sector is unable to meet the challenge associated with the demands of a nonaffluent group, and that inability is abetted by the actions of the public sector which has been active in the removal of housing in the areas where adequate housing is most sorely needed.[35]

[35] Housing and Urban Development Legislation of 1970, Hearing before the Subcommittee on Housing and Urban Affairs, Ninety-First Congress, U.S. Government Printing Office, Washington, D.C., 1970, p. 811.

Continued ghettoization further aggravates the problem thereby creating greater dissatisfaction and increasing the level of frustration within that population. Newark, New Jersey, whose population is now predominantly black, was the only major city in the nation in 1970 which issued fewer than 20 permits for new housing construction inside the central city. Even St. Louis, which recorded the largest relative decline of population in its central-city population during the sixties, issued permits for more than 300 new units.[36] While the owner occupancy rate of black home owners is on the increase in those cities which are essentially single family housing cities, this fact should not be allowed to shield the problem of the growing housing crisis in ghettos throughout the nation. The problem of urban black population growth is first reflected in housing, but tends to fan out from this base into all aspects of urban living.

36 *Housing Authorized by Building Permits and Public Contracts,* U.S. Department of Commerce, Bureau of the Census, April, 1971, Government Printing Office, Washington, D.C.

CHAPTER 3

GHETTO ECONOMIC CHARACTERISTICS

The economic characteristics alone prevailing in the nation's ghettos set them aside as unique territorial units within urban America. The low level of economic development universally associated with these entities is implicit in their conceptual identity. Although some writers make the distinction between ghettos which are defined in terms of economics and those defined in terms of race,[1] these are seldom mutually exclusive entities.

In attempting to specify the economic characteristics of the ghetto from a geographic perspective, one must view this problem in terms of both its people component as well as its place component, for the two are in reality inseparable. The obvious manifestations of limited economic development associated with elements of place are in large measure a reflection of the economic status of a large segment of the residential population. But one could likewise demonstrate that economic status of the population is bound up in selective aspects of place which vary in importance in terms of relative location within the metropolitan system. On the other hand, a process-oriented approach might look at how the ghetto economy operates and what its impact is on the aforementioned state. The latter approach was employed recently by Fusfeld to great advantage.[2] The weakness of this approach revolves around the fact that the ghetto economic state is less affected by the operation of its local economy than it is by the larger metropolitan economy.

---

[1] Anthony Downs, "Alternatives for the American Ghetto," *Daedalus,* Fall, 1968, p. 1331.
[2] Daniel Fusfeld, "The Economy of the Urban Ghetto," in John P. Crecine, ed., *Financing the Metropolis,* Sage Publications, Beverly Hills, Calif., 1970, p. 374.

GHETTO RESOURCES

Ghetto economic characteristics can be placed in proper perspective by investigating the nature of the productive and consumptive forces which operate within the ghetto context. Of the various factors contributing to the production of goods and services, there is only one which tends to be found in quantity within the ghetto—manpower. It is frequently said that, of all the investment resources which might be employed to stimulate production, manpower is the only ghetto resource which is not scarce. While manpower represents an abundant resource in an absolute sense, the problem when viewed from a different perspective, partially alters our previous claim. The inability to match the manpower resources in the ghetto with available employment opportunities existing within the metropolitan system leads to a neutralization of manpower resources and creates a condition of relative scarcity curbing productive potential. Thus, the most obvious ghetto resource, it turns out, is hardly a resource that can be invested in the production of goods and services that promote positive feedback for ghetto areas.

The difficulty of transforming much of the manpower potential lodged within the ghetto into the kind of productive skills which the national industrial apparatus tends to reward, leads to the development of an adjustment mechanism which fosters and promotes the operation of what Fusfeld chooses to describe as the irregular economy.[3] The irregular economy is generally associated with the production of goods and services for local ghetto consumption, many of which represent activities which are illegal or of questionable legality. The benefits which accrue from the operation of the irregular economy, while tending to enhance the financial status of a very small segment of this manpower pool, contribute very little toward altering the economic characteristics of most ghetto residents. Conversely, the irregular economy does contribute toward placing the ghetto under constant surveillance and thereby partially validates ghetto residents' claims of police occupation.

Not only is effective manpower a scarce resource in the ghetto, a condition which must be altered if the ghetto is ever to be transformed into a viable community rather than a behavioral sink, there is also often absent the machinery of production necessary to transform raw materials into marketable products. The above generalization reflects the continuous decline of job opportunites within the existing ghetto territorial configuration since World War II. The loss of manufacturing jobs within easy access of ghetto residential areas has hit hardest at the potential for moving out of a condition of

[3] *Ibid.*

poverty[4] and into the category of working and middle-income peoples.   Thus, seldom are goods-processing firms indigenous to the ghetto, but increasingly those firms, which in some quarters are viewed as extraterritorial, are abandoning the ghetto for economically and physically more attractive sites within the metropolitan system.

There is little doubt that evidence of this sort leads the government to give attention to the concept of black capitalism. But the kind of structural changes required to offset fleeing economic opportunity cannot be accomplished by the promotion of the brand of capitalism that has obviously been chosen as appropriate, and is represented by firms that might be given birth through loans from the Small Business Administration. Efforts of this type would aid an insignificant number of small businessmen and would hardly change the ghetto's economic characteristics. One might anticipate efforts of this sort to have some of the same kinds of payoffs that come from the operation of the irregular economy, except that such efforts would probably not generate increased surveillance.

It is becoming increasingly evident that the ghetto is evolving into a configuration devoid of meaningful employment opportunities, and at the same time is becoming the place of residence of persons with limited employment potential. It is obvious that the latter condition is less intractable than the former, given the absence of major changes in the manner in which the economy operates. The likelihood of increasing employment opportunities within the production sector of the economy appears to be rather bleak, even though there are moves afoot which are designed to promote the development of goods-producing units within the ghetto. While some limited successes have been recorded in this regard, they have not been of sufficient magnitude to do more than maintain the status quo. The ghetto, then, is rapidly becoming a dormitory, and the distance between workplace and place of residence is continually increasing. But more important than that is the nature of the jobs which are tending to become more physically remote from the ghetto location.

THE GHETTO WORKER

The accumulation of manpower resources in the area designated as the ghetto reflects the vision of a people for heightened economic opportunity. Few would question the strength of economic factors in promoting movement from areas of limited economic opportunity

[4] Joseph B. Mooney, "Housing Segregation, Negro Employment, and Metropolitan Decentralization: An Alternative Perspective," *Quarterly Journal of Economics*, May, 1969, pp. 310-311.

to areas of increasing economic opportunity, and ghetto growth and development partially reflect the strength of this force. It was during periods in our recent history when jobs were most abundant that the streams of black migration emanating from the South were choked with future ghetto residents. Both World War I and World War II created the need for unlimited manpower and an ever-increasing number of black people responded to the call.

Today's ghetto manpower pool represents second- and third-generation offspring of those persons who envisioned increased economic opportunity to be associated with the trek from the countryside to the city. To these have been recently added many others who were pushed rather than pulled into the nation's leading ghetto centers. That most of the nation's urban black manpower pool is ghetto-located is obvious, and even though a number of black workers are not residents of the ghetto, until recently a large number of the ghetto escapees were linked to the ghetto through employment. In the past, the most frequent escapee of the ghetto was the black professional who quite often plied his trade in the ghetto. Thus black people located both inside and outside of the ghetto territorial configuration make up part of the ghetto work force.

The Composition of the Work Force

The composition of the black work force is still overwhelmingly unskilled, although the proportion of workers classified as semiskilled is on the increase. As recently as 1969, 72 percent of all black labor force participants were in the combined blue-collar worker/service worker category. Changes are occurring which indicate that an increasing number of black workers are moving into white-collar occupations. The greatest progress has been made in the occupational categories of professional and technical workers and clerical workers. Likewise, there has been a large-scale decline in the number of black workers classified as laborers and private household workers.

Within the blue-collar category, blacks have had the least success in entering the category of craftsmen, the most highly remunerative category within the blue-collar group, regularly exceeding the average pay received by those in lower-order white-collar jobs. The decline in the number and proportion of laborers and private household workers is in part associated with changes in technology and secondarily associated with changes in region of residence. In 1960 approximately one-third of all black, female, labor-force participants in the nation were in the private household worker category,[5] and within some large Southern cities the proportion exceeded 70 percent. A younger generation of black women is increasingly finding

[5] Herman P. Miller, *Rich Man, Poor Man*, Crowell, New York, 1964, pp. 93-94.

its way into jobs in the clerical field, the principal employment category of all females in the labor force.

Black males have made limited progress in establishing themselves in the crafts, but the task has been tedious and barriers yet remain. In 1960 a disproportionate number of black craftsmen were employed in crafts that were designated "Negro occupations."[6] For the most part, the black migrant to the Northern ghetto has had to accept less stable jobs in the less remunerative operative category. Within big city ghettos, black males are heavily engaged in the performance of operative-type jobs, of which truck drivers and delivery men represent the principal archetype. Black women, for a variety of reasons, including higher general level of educational attainment, have made greater progress in eliminating barriers to more meaningful employment opportunities than have black males.

Spatial Variations in the Black Occupational Structure

Spatial differentiation on the basis of occupational status is less evident within the ghetto than it is outside. Nevertheless, some spatial differentiation based on occupational status can be detected. At the neighborhood level within individual ghettos, the predominance of various combinations of occupational groupings is somewhat evident. In many lower-income black neighborhoods, the work force is principally composed of laborers and operatives or service workers and operatives. Moving from lower-income neighborhoods to working-class neighborhoods, the occupational structure is likely to reflect an increased proportion of craftsmen or is likely to be best described as diversified in terms of the occupational mix. There are few ghetto neighborhoods in which there exists a preponderance of white-collar workers. A disproportionate ratio of white-collar workers and craftsmen added to an operative majority can and does produce the vast majority of middle-income neighborhoods within ghetto areas. The strength of the private household employment sector is revealed in some Southern cities, since that occupational group is frequently represented in ghetto neighborhoods. No attempt has been made here to rigorously identify ghetto neighborhoods on the basis of occupational status, but crude attempts to identify neighborhoods on this basis, employing some sort of quantitative index, have previously been undertaken.

Employment Status of the Ghetto Labor Force

Ghetto neighborhoods are most often viewed in terms of the problematic aspects of their employment status. Unemployment as

---

[6] Daniel O. Price, *Changing Characteristics of the Negro Population,* U.S. Department of Commerce, Washington, D.C., 1969, p. 145.

well as underemployment in ghetto neighborhoods exceeds that of almost all other neighborhoods to be found within cities. The "normal" black-white unemployment ratio in the United States is approximately 2:1. At no time since 1955 has the ratio dropped below this so-called normal level, which simply turns out to be a long-time average and seemingly an expected pattern. Thus, in terms of employment rates the situation grew steadily worse for the ghetto resident after World War II, but began to settle out at the 2:1 level after 1955. While the ratio of black-to-white employment has remained fairly steady, there has been much fluctuation in the absolute level of employment of ghetto populations over most of this period.

A survey of Cleveland's poverty neighborhoods in 1966 revealed that 47 percent of all families were partially supported by transfer payments (unemployment insurance, general welfare, aid to dependent children, etc.).[7] Today, as the national level of unemployment hovers ever closer to the 6 percent level, this means that ghetto neighborhoods can be assumed to have entered a period of extreme crisis. The combination of persistent high levels of unemployment and low levels of remuneration, given the prevailing occupational characteristic of ghetto areas, creates widespread poverty within the ghetto.

THE EXTENT OF GHETTO POVERTY

In 1968, 20 percent of all black families were receiving incomes that placed them in the poverty category. Ten years earlier, almost half of the nation's black families were below the poverty level. The nature and seriousness of the problem prompted the Department of Labor to attempt to delineate poverty neighborhoods in central cities within the Standard Metropolitan Statistical Areas (SMSA) containing more than 250,000 people. The criteria employed in delineating poverty areas were as follows: (1) family income below $3,000; (2) children in broken homes; (3) persons of low educational attainment; (4) males in unskilled jobs; (5) substandard housing.

It is obvious from the foregoing that poverty areas were not identified purely on economic grounds. Thus it appears that the territorial units described as poverty areas by the Department of Labor are areas which some writers would describe as neighborhoods characterized by a culture of poverty. Since agencies concerned with the problems of poverty often operate on the assumption that it is necessary to change the behavior of the target population as a prelude to the elimination of poverty, then the basis for delineating poverty areas in this manner is made clear. On the other hand, it is

[7] Fusfeld, *op. cit.*

rather unfortunate that a public agency would stigmatize a segment of space on what appears to represent an economic basis when, in fact, it includes at least one social component. Furthermore, it has been pointed out previously that a sizable number of people residing in poverty areas are not characterized by poverty, using a strict definition of poverty.

Recently Mooney attempted to identify poverty areas in the 52 largest SMSAs in the nation.[8] In defining poverty areas, Mooney chose as a criterion those census tracts in which the median family income of the tract was two-thirds or less than the median family income in the SMSA. Mooney was inclined to describe these areas as ghettos, but not in a racial sense. Nevertheless, more than 60 percent of all poverty areas identified using the Mooney criteria were predominantly black. The advantage of the Mooney technique lies in its simplicity; the ease with which it can be employed in comparing the extent of poverty areas; and its definition of poverty as a relative economic state predicated on a local economic base.

A recent attempt to distinguish zones within the ghetto that would illustrate spatial variations in the economic status of black populations was conducted by this writer, using a slight modification of the Mooney technique. Lower income areas were identified in precisely the same fashion that Mooney employed to distinguish poverty areas, but with a single exception, that being the substitution of central-city median family income for that of the SMSA. Those census tracts in which the median family income of the nonwhite residents was less than 90 percent but greater than 66 percent of the city's median family income were identified as working-class areas. When the median family income within a tract equaled or exceeded 90 percent of the city's median, the area was identified as a middle-class area. This tripartite identity structure was defined solely on economic grounds and therefore produces results that are incongruent with those developed by the Department of Labor.

It becomes readily obvious that the zones described as the poverty area by the Federal government are much more extensive in the cities investigated than are the poverty or lower (income) class neighborhoods as defined via the modified Mooney technique. The results of the two methods can be observed, as they have been applied to 1960 data from Milwaukee, Wisconsin, and Denver, Colorado (Figures 3.1 and 3.2). Of the 23 neighborhoods which made up the Milwaukee ghetto in 1960, only 8 were identified as low-income areas using the modified Mooney technique, whereas

[8] Joseph B. Mooney, op. cit., pp. 308-310

only 2 of the neighborhoods fell outside of the Department of Labor's poverty area. It is readily obvious that Milwaukee's poverty area, as defined on a nonstrict economic basis, is much more extensive than the area defined as the black ghetto. A similar phenomenon prevails in Denver. In both instances most of the neighborhoods identified as working-class areas, using a strict economic measure, show up as poverty areas when government criteria are employed.

Figure 3.1   Milwaukee's poverty area, 1960.

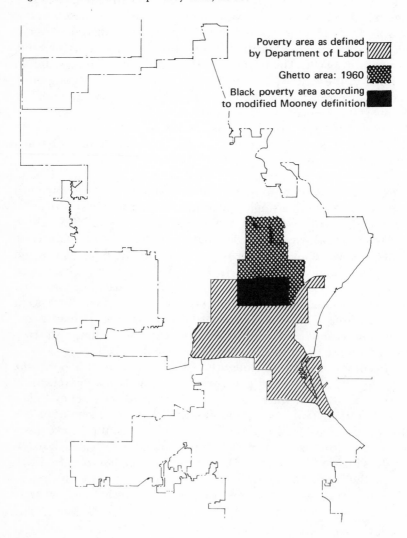

Figure 3.2   Denver's poverty area, 1960.

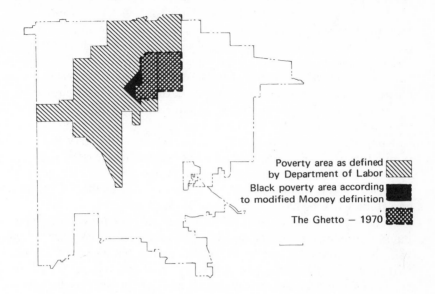

Poverty area as defined
by Department of Labor

Black poverty area according
to modified Mooney definition

The Ghetto — 1970

Employment Conditions within Ghetto Poverty Areas

The Department of Labor's increasing interest in big-city poverty areas has recently resulted in the reporting of economic conditions in those areas, a situation that did not previously exist. Beginning in 1966 information on the unemployment level within poverty areas in the 100 largest SMSAs was reported. Previously the level of unemployment was reported for individual cities and did not take note of variations in the level of employment within subareas of cities. During that year, while the national unemployment level hovered around 3.8 percent, the level prevailing in Cleveland's Hough area, Phoenix's Salt River Bed area, Oakland's Bayside area, and St. Louis' Northside area, ghettos all, were 15.8, 13.2, 13.0, and 12.9 percent respectively.[9] Thus, in several of the nation's ghetto areas the 1966 unemployment rates indicated a worsening trend, while for the nation as a whole the employment picture was becoming brighter.

As of 1968 the Department of Labor began collecting detailed information on employment conditions in six of the nation's most extreme poverty areas. These are subareas within the larger poverty

[9] Shirley A. Goetz, "Unemployment in Philadelphia," *Philadelphia Federal Reserve,* Feb., 1968, pp. 6-7.

areas previously defined for these cities. The cities for which there is detailed information on the employment situation prevailing during 1968 and 1969 are as follows: Houston, Atlanta, Los Angeles, Detroit, Chicago, and New York. In some cities, the areas of extreme poverty are represented by a single spatial cluster and in others as series of noncontiguous spatial clusters. In Houston, Detroit, and Chicago, the most severe problems of poverty are situated in a single cluster, whereas in New York and Los Angeles noncontiguous spatial clusters prevail. Black ghetto areas constitute a major share of each single cluster zone. In all areas, however, the racial composition of the population is mixed. Only in the Chicago poverty area is the population overwhelmingly black. The results of this survey go a long way in spelling out the nature of economic well-being of that segment of the black population which resides in the lower-income and some working-class segments of the ghetto.

There is a good deal of variation in the prevailing level of unemployment among the six recently surveyed poverty areas. These variations indicate differences in the general employment situation within individual cities, the principal economic function of these cities, and the occupational characteristics of the poverty population. Among these six areas, the extreme positions along the employment spectrum are represented by Detroit and New York City. The Detroit poverty area in 1969 was characterized by an unemployment rate of 12.2 percent, while New York City's level was 6.8 percent. The remaining four areas had unemployment levels ranging between 8 and 10.3 percent. The Detroit and New York situations clearly highlight the distinct economic functions which characterize these places and thus their corresponding occupational structure. More than 25 percent of all black workers in the New York poverty area were classified as white-collar workers during 1968 and 1969, while in Detroit only slightly more than 11 percent of such workers were found in this category. The overwhelming concentrations of black workers in the blue-collar occupations (77.1 percent) and in a single industrial class help explain the Detroit situation. New York, with a more balanced distribution of employment among the principal occupational categories, is less sensitive to the economic fluctuations which tend to strike a single sector of the economy.

The most severe level of unemployment in these areas is that associated with the segment of the population between sixteen and nineteen years of age. In each of these areas the unemployment level is in excess of 25 percent, ranging from 25.3 percent in New York to 36.4 percent in Detroit. It is the high incidence of unemployment within this age group that is frequently cited as providing the fuel for social explosion within ghetto areas. Black ghetto workers situated

outside "hard-core poverty areas" enjoy lower levels of unemployment, but nevertheless the level is always higher than that prevailing
in the city as a whole (Table 3.1).

Table 3.1 Level of unemployment in poverty areas and the central city for
selected cities by race, 1968-1969

Place	City unemployment rate (%)	Poverty area unemployment rate		City unemployment rate	
		black	white	black	white
Detroit	5.5	13.5	9.1	8.5	3.9
Los Angeles	5.9	15.2	6.3	8.0	4.8
Atlanta	—	9.4	5.3	—	—
Chicago	3.4	8.8	4.0	5.9	2.6
Houston	3.2	9.5	5.9	6.6	2.1
New York City	3.5	6.7	6.9	4.7	3.3

Source: *Poverty—The Broad Outline, Detroit,* Urban Employment Survey, Report No. 1,
U.S. Department of Labor, February, 1970; "Geographic Aspects of Unemployment in 1969," *News,* U.S. Department of Labor, April 6, 1970.

It is obvious that even within poverty areas there is considerable
variation in the work status of the population along racial lines.
These variations are not solely confined to unemployment levels, but
show up in labor force participation rates, occupational structure,
and industry of employment. Some of these conditions are related to
differentials in the level of achieved characteristics of the population,
others to cultural and social attributes, and others to the obstacles or
barriers to black employment which is an outgrowth of attitudes
prevailing in the larger society. For instance, in those three cities
where the poverty areas are shared by blacks and persons of Spanish
origin, such as in Los Angeles, Houston, and New York City, the
labor force participation rate of black women is considerably higher
than that prevailing among females having been socialized within a
Latin culture. This phenomenon is largely evident among the married
female sector of the population, that is, black married women are
much more likely to be members of the labor force than are Latin
women.

Within New York's poverty areas the labor force participation
rate prevailing during the survey period for black women was 57
percent, while that for Puerto Rican women was only 30 percent. A
similar phenomenon was observed in Houston, with the level of black
female participation set at 61.3 percent, while the prevailing level for
women of Spanish heritage was 37 percent. When "other" white
women are found in poverty areas, their labor force participation
rates are higher than those of white women of Spanish background.

The higher labor force participation rates for these women reflects in part an older age structure and a high percentage of female-headed households.

It should be pointed out there that while the various poverty areas tend to be composed of members of various racial and ethnic groups, each group tends to reside within a segment of that space where members of his group are in the majority, although in some instances the black ghetto, Spanish barrio, and the white enclave are spatially contiguous (Figure 3.3). They most often represent communities which are socially separate. On the contrary, the two major poverty areas in Los Angeles are spatially noncontiguous. The Mexican-American barrio is generally referred to as the East Los Angeles poverty area, whereas that segment of the black ghetto which constitutes the alternate poverty zone is referred to as the South Los Angeles poverty area. The latter area encompasses much of the community of Watts.

Figure 3.3   Houston's poverty zone, 1960. (Source: *Poverty in Houston's Central City*, Regional Report Series #1, U.S. Department of Labor, Feb., 1970)

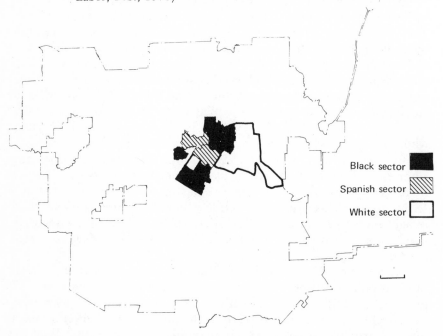

Black sector
Spanish sector
White sector

Another glaring disparity within this select set of poverty areas is the extent to which black women tend to be household heads. In most instances, no fewer than 32 percent of the households are headed by females. In the New York poverty complex, almost half of all households are headed by females. This condition severely affects the economic character of the area of residence. Given the nature of the employment opportunities available to black women and the level of remuneration associated with them, a situation of permanent poverty can be envisioned. In Houston, Atlanta, and Chicago, approximately one-third of all female labor force participants are involved in private household employment. The level of private household employment in the remaining cities is nearer the 20 percent level. But in all instances, black women are concentrated in low-level service occupations.

There are signs which indicate black women are beginning to gain greater access to higher level service type jobs in New York City than was previously the case. As there has been a major overhaul in New York City's employment structure during the past decade, with service jobs coming to dominate the employment picture, the employment situation for black women has improved. While the situation has favored the black female, it has worked to the disadvantage of the black male, who must now chase the manufacturing jobs to the suburbs or withdraw from the labor force. Black women from New York City's poverty areas do not appear to have benefited to the same extent from the city's changing industrial structure as have women located outside the poverty zones. Hiestand, in describing the improvements made by minority members in New York's work force, indicated that a number of barriers to continued improvements yet exist.[10] The barriers Hiestand cited are as follows: (1) union domination of skilled jobs which are considered the private preserve of white ethnics; (2) the traditional lack of receptivity to change on the part of the city's high prestige organizations and agencies which deal with them; (3) the unchanging hiring practices of the small firms located throughout the city; (4) barriers to management posts in general; and (5) barriers to the better sales positions. It is obvious, then, that even within an enlightened social environment the dual job market prevails.

The Nonworking Segment of the Ghetto Population

Many of the nation's social commentators are more inclined to focus their attention on that segment of the manpower pool that is found outside the labor force. Among the residents of poverty areas, this segment of the population frequently accounts for as many as one-third of all persons sixteen years of age and older. These are persons who have often dropped out of the labor force because of ill

[10] Dale H. Hiestand, "Equal Employment in New York City," *Industrial Relations,* May, 1970, p. 303.

health, age, family responsibility, or discouagement. The latter cause
leads to these persons receiving such labels as the "hard-core
unemployed." Members of this small but growing population constitute one segment of the population of dependency. Some writers
have labeled this segment of the manpower pool as pathological and
assert that none of the programs which have been designed to place
them in jobs are likely to produce the expected results. It is said that
these persons possess a lower-class culture which conditions their
outlook on life, an outlook that is antithetical to middle-class goals.
While easy explanations of this sort might permit the nonpoor sector
of the population some satisfaction in that it supports their previously held notions, it does not come to grips with the problem in a
realistic fashion.

The politics of poverty, or the games people play in attempting
to deal with the problem, frequently create a new set of problems
without resolving those problems for which poverty programs were
developed. Unfortunately, for that large segment of the working
poor who share a common physical space with the nonworking poor,
the problems of the latter bear down hard on the daily life of the
former. Thus, even in Detroit's most severe poverty area, the average
black family can be described as a member of the lower working
class. The poverty designation which defines their area of residence
in large measure reflects the existence of a set of social qualities
which are thought to be problem provoking. Outside of Detroit's
poverty area the average black family of two or more persons can be
described as lower middle class and the average family of four or
more persons falls into the category of upper working class. Thus,
most adult ghetto residents are actively involved in earning their
daily bread and acquiring the many gadgets that the American
industrial system produces. That their earnings permit them only
limited access to the goods and services that are available in the
marketplace does not require substantiation.

ECONOMIC DEVELOPMENT IN THE GHETTO

The previous set of descriptions of the ghetto worker are principally
ecological, as they represent aggregate descriptions of the employment characteristics based on areal data. The interrelatedness of
people and place are highlighted when information is structured in
this way, although social scientists are aware of the danger of
generalizing at the level of the individual from ecological data. The
principal task which remains in an attempt to untangle a complex
web is to partition the people/place component of the ghetto
economy. The resident population of the spatial unit termed the
ghetto possesses the set of economic characteristics described in the

previous sections, but the capital-producing agents which serve as the economic support base for the ghetto are seldom located within that territorial configuration, and even when these agents possess a ghetto location, they do not serve the ghetto community directly.

The political structure of American cities makes it impossible for capital-producing agents to provide direct economic support to social areas within cities that constitute something less than an independent political entity. Thus, to speak of the ghetto economy is no doubt technically inaccurate, since capital generated in the ghetto is not earmarked to provide economic support for the ghetto as a territorial entity. The income derived by the vast majority of ghetto residents is earned through employment at workplaces located beyond the ghetto, and when ghetto-located, these workplaces are operated by persons or firms that are not ghetto-based. This situation, it is alleged, has led to a condition of both people-poverty and place-poverty.

Place-Poverty and Ghetto Development

The place-poverty aspects of the "ghetto economy," then, are largely associated with the absence of effective capital-producing units within the ghetto which could alter the condition of the ghetto environment by providing it with greater financial support. This has led to a call for increased support for ghetto business. It is often pointed out in the literature that black Americans are largely devoid of an entrepreneurial heritage, and thus ghetto business is dominated by other Americans. It has been estimated that blacks own only 5 percent of the business in those communities with 50,000 or more blacks.[11] Even in those instances where ghetto businesses are owned by blacks, they tend to be economically marginal with little potential for providing opportunities for employment.

It appears that the increasing support for black business that has become pronounced during the last three years is an attempt to create a contingent of small independent businessmen who will be largely protected against the possibility of failure. The small entrepreneur was the backbone of American business success in a prior era, but to use him as a model would represent an open admission that the ghetto is a quasi-economic unit, which is at a different stage along the spectrum of economic development than most of urban America. If this represents an acceptable premise, how does one bridge the chronological gap in economic development terms between the two urban Americas? Some see the answer in black

11 Sar A. Levitan, Garth L. Mangum, and Robert Taggart III, *Economic Opportunity in the Ghetto: The Partnership of Government and Business,* The Johns Hopkins University Press, Baltimore, Md., 1970, p. 5.

capitalism of the sort mentioned above, but black capitalism has come under criticism from a wide variety of critics. These criticisms are often social as well as economic in nature. Nevertheless, if black capitalism does nothing more than point up the problems that are believed to be an outgrowth of place-poverty, it will have focused on an aspect of the problem that is frequently neglected. Now that these wheels have been placed in motion, it is possible that a degree of economic transformation will follow that is designed to add to the capital-producing stock within the ghetto and ultimately lead to capital retention as a means of altering the quality of services available to its residents.

The existing variations on the theme of black capitalism (or, better still, the more valid concept of black economic development) revolve around how the various strategies perceive the ghetto as an economic unit within both the national and metropolitan economies. The positions assumed on this topic tend to vary as a function of any one or combination of the following attributes: (a) race; (b) social class; (c) representatives of the private sector; and/or (d) representatives of the public sector. Increasingly, there is evidence which suggests that there are elements in the black community which view the black ghetto as a semidetached, quasi-independent entity that requires a productive enconomic base, with the community possessing some measure of control over the capital generated by this heightened productive power. Representatives from those sectors of the national administrative machinery who are responsible for maintaining the economy in sound working order tend to have a less expansive view of the role of economic development within the ghetto context. The combination of the attributes mentioned above leaves room for a wide range of perceptions of the type of economic development that is in the best interest of the ghetto, the city, the metropolitan area, and the nation.

Local blacks who are concerned with community development increasingly view the problem as one of place-poverty and tend to be strong advocates of ghetto economic development, while whites representing both the private and public sectors tend to view the situation as one of people-poverty and see the provision of additional jobs as the key to the solution of the problem. While this is an oversimplification of this two-dimensional view, it does represent the principal points of departure toward the promotion of solutions to the problem of ghetto poverty and economic discrimination. The notion of community economic development received increased currency during the period immediately following the series of long, hot summers.

In 1968, the Community Self-Determination Bill was introduced in the Senate, and if it had been passed, it would have defined a territorial unit within the ghetto that would have possessed a measure of control over those economic units operating within that space. The Community Self-Determination Bill was principally the work of two of the nation's chief architects of black economic development, Roy Innis and Floyd McKissick. While the arguments incorporated in the bill appeared to appeal initially to a broad spectrum of political philosophies, much of the appeal was lost as arguments against the bill began to mount. The principal opposition to the bill revolved around the power to be invested in the Community Development Corporation. If Senate Bill 3876 had been passed, it would have given local black territorial communities extensive powers in the area of economic self-determination. Accusations which stated that the bill fostered separatism and placed white owned and operated firms in a disadvantageous position dampened support for it. Sturdivant, in his criticism of the bill, had this to say: [12]

Community development corporations would perpetuate the inefficient fragmented commercial and industrial structure of slum areas. Most low-income urban areas are characterized by the virtual absence of a manufacturing base and by a retail community made up largely of small, independent stores.

In support of the basic mechanics of the bill is a statement by one of its architects:[13]

Blacks must innovate, must create a new ideology. It may include elements of capitalism, elements of socialism, or elements of neither; that is immaterial. What matters is that it will be created to fit our needs. So then black people are not talking about black capitalism. Black people are talking about economic development. We are talking about the creation and acquisition of capital instruments by means of which to maximize our economic interests. We do not particularly try to define styles of ownership; we say that we are willing to operate pragmatically and let the style of ownership fit the style of the area of its inhabitants.

It is now believed that the Community Self-Determination Bill has little chance of attracting enough support for its passage. The enthusiasm shown for it by the 90th Congress had been lost on the 91st Congress.

---

[12] Frederick D. Sturdivant, "The Limits of Black Capitalism," *Harvard Business Review*, Jan.-Feb., 1969, p. 123.
[13] Roy Innis, "Separatists Economics: A New Social Contract," in William F. Haddad and G. Douglas Pugh, eds., *Black Economic Development*, Prentice-Hall, Englewood Cliffs, N.J., pp. 52-53.

The unique Community Development Corporation idea which was the central element in the proposed Community Self-Determination Bill has simply faded away as a nonrational construct. But Community Development Corporations (CDCs) without the power that would have been granted them under the provision of the Community Self-Determination Bill are growing in number and have come into existence in a wide variety of ghetto communities. It was recently estimated that there now exist some 70 CDCs in the nation.[14] The Community Development Corporation usually represents a nonprofit organization which uses its skills to attract capital and expertise into the black community for the purpose of promoting the development and establishment of profit corporations within the ghetto. To date, the support of the local CDCs has been varied and has come from both the private and public sectors. Even though the Community Self-Determination Bill was not acted upon by the Congress, some CDCs are supported by funds made available through the Office of Economic Opportunity under Title 1-D of the Economic Opportunity Act. Given the variations in the source of financial support and the structure of local CDCs, it was recently suggested that they might be classified in the following way:[15] (1) establishment-dominated organizations; (2) minority-initiated and controlled organizations; and (3) shared-leadership organizations.

There exist examples of each of these CDC types spawning successful business enterprises within the ghetto context. FIGHTON, a black corporation manufacturing electrical transformers for Xerox, owes its existence to the efforts of the Rochester Business Opportunity Council (RBOC), a type-one CDC. Progress Plaza, a shopping center in north Philadelphia, is an outgrowth of the efforts of Reverend Leon Sullivan's 10/36 program, a type-two CDC. A kind of dual but quasi-independent council constitutes the structure of type-three CDCs. Within the framework of this set of CDCs, a number of major firms have developed businesses in the ghetto that produce a wide variety of products. Those firms whose ghetto plants produce components that can be utilized in other units of a firm's manufacturing complex have tended to have the greatest success. IBM's Bedford-Stuyvesant plant is generally hailed as one of the most successful operations to date. In contrast, those firms that had not engaged in careful planning and chose to produce items for which they had no captive market have suffered financial losses. The Watts manufacturing firm which came into existence in 1966 as a result of action initiated by Aero-Jet General fits into the latter category.

[14] Arthur I. Blaustein, "What Is Community Economic Development?", *Urban Affairs Quarterly*, Sept., 1970, p. 60.
[15] Levitan, et al., *op. cit.*, pp. 75-78.

General Motors has recently come to the rescue of the Watts Manufacturing Company by subcontracting with them to produce glove compartment components.[16]

At least a dozen major corporations are presently involved in developing ghetto businesses. The firms created provide employment for black workers who in many instances are described as members of the hard-core unemployed. The ultimate disposition of all ghetto firms is unclear at this time, but there is evidence that some firms intend to divest themselves of their ghetto holdings by permitting their employees to purchase stock in them or by simply transferring ownership to an agent of the black community. If a larger number of the nation's top industrial and nonindustrial firms become involved in the process of developing business enterprises in the ghetto, the conditions of the place-poverty might be greatly ameliorated. The noble efforts of a few firms, though, can hardly be expected to turn the tide. It has been pointed out that the willingness of businesses to become involved in ghetto development efforts in large measure reflects what some firms perceive as being in their general best interest. Firms with extensive capital holdings in the ghetto or in the central city in general tend to have a higher performance record in this area than firms whose holdings tend to be located outside the central city. It should also be remembered that some firms are induced to participate in ghetto development programs in response to the availability of governmental subsidies designed for such purposes.

JOB LOCATION AND PEOPLE-POVERTY

The previous discussion of place-poverty and the role economic development might play in ameliorating that situation should not be allowed to obscure our view of changes occurring within the larger metropolitan system, which imposes hardships upon the individual black worker in his attempt to escape from a situation of poverty or quasipoverty. There is little doubt that the individual black worker is more concerned with his particular economic plight than with the conditions prevailing within a territorial community. Nevertheless, many analysts view this problem as a dual one. Of course Spratlen was correct in his criticism of a colleague who tended to emphasize the singular importance of community economic development when he stated:[17]

16 *Ibid.,* p. 12.
17 Thaddeus H. Spratlen, "A Black Perspective on Black Business Development," *Journal of Marketing,* Oct., 1970, p. 72.

If, as the author suggests, business ownership and management have replaced employment as "the number one priority issue" facing the black community, the rationale has to be political rhetoric rather than economic reality. Even if the relative magnitudes of black enterprise could be tripled over its present levels, such a statement would still be dubious from an economic point of view.

There is little doubt that the availability of jobs is of paramount importance to the unemployed and underemployed ghetto worker. Jobs which attracted a previous generation of black workers to the central city are becoming increasingly scarce as life in the ghetto becomes increasingly dismal. The ghetto environment itself has deteriorated, and employment centers once located in the ghetto or near the margins of the ghetto have abandoned these locations in favor of sites which provide a greater number of economies and more attractive and accessible environments.

The Changing Geography of Workplace Locations

Kain recently enumerated the changes which occurred in the location of economic activity within the 40 largest SMSAs in the nation during the period 1948-1963.[18] During this period the largest central cities in the nation lost thousands of jobs to their suburban rings. The decentralization of employment has hit hardest that segment of the population with the fewest skills and the least access to new job locations, the ghetto worker. Of the four major job categories used by the Census of Business, the changes which have occurred within the manufacturing group reflect the greatest hardships on the ghetto worker, for it was this category of employment that included the previous low-income groups in industrial America who had rid themselves of the shackles of poverty. Kain reports that, during the period 1954-1963, the central cities in his samples each lost on the average approximately 25,000 manufacturing jobs, while the suburban rings gained an approximately equal number.[19] It thus becomes apparent that what previously ranked as a principal source of employment for a segment of the ghetto population was locating beyond the domain of ghetto labor-force entrants. Of the four major employment categories previously mentioned, only selected services showed an increase in central-city employment over this 15-year interval. Thus, increasingly, service type jobs characterized by limited remuneration have represented the only stable sources of employment for ghetto males.

[18] John F. Kain, "The Distribution and Movement of Jobs and Industry," in James Q. Wilson ed., *The Metropolitan Enigma*, Harvard University Press, Cambridge, Mass., 1968, pp. 16-17.
[19] *Ibid.*

The central cities of the nation have become more and more the domain of the white-collar worker. This alteration of the employment locational structure has provided some benefits for black females, as clerical opportunities have become more numerous as a result of changes both in terms of physical and social access. Residual retail opportunities have likewise been expanded as major retailers have decentralized in pursuit of a suburbanizing population, thus reducing competition for jobs in Central Business District complexes. Jobs remaining in the central city tend to be concentrated in the less desirable sectors of industry and/or the nongrowth sectors.

Many blacks are securely employed in firms possessing central-city locations and even ghetto locations, but the possibility of these firms or individual units being able to adequately absorb new entrants to the labor force is remote. This condition largely is expressed in the high rate of unemployment among blacks in the 16 to 29 age groups. The availability of employment opportunities for young blacks possessing limited skills is partially conditioned by the geography of work location and the attitudes of employers within the metropolitan system.

Frequently small firms located in areas undergoing racial change run into difficult adjustment problems in dealing with the possibility of hiring black workers. These attitudes often represent the inability of personnel officers to overcome a tradition of racial exclusion or a response to the perceived attitudes of the existing work force. In one instance the adjustment problem was handled by locating the employment office of a ghetto-located plant in another sector of the community as a means of discouraging ghetto applicants. These kinds of practices, though, only increase the antagonisms between ghetto residents and ghetto-located firms. But even if the problem of discrimination in the workplace were completely eliminated, the problems that have arisen as a result of mobile jobs and immobile people would still be with us.

Black Worker Access to Jobs

The absolute magnitude of this problem has not been detailed, as the few researchers who have shown an interest in the problem have been restricted in their efforts by the nature and availability of data. Those researchers who have attempted to investigate the problem as it pertains to a number of metropolitan areas at some common point in time have frequently been forced to make use of aggregate data detailing changes occurring between the central city and the suburban ring area. A few researchers have undertaken detailed studies for individual places. Thus we are placed in a position to generalize about conditions prevailing over a relatively large number of places from gross data, or to make general statements about a universe of places deduced from detailed analysis of a single place. Kain hypothesized that black residential segregation negatively affected the black worker's opportunities to secure employment in the employment growth zones within a metropolitan system.[20]

A more detailed spatial analytic approach to this general problem was recently undertaken by Deskins, who wished to ascertain if the Kain hypothesis was valid over time. Deskins chose to test the Kain hypothesis by specifying the changing nature of the journey-to-work pattern for black and white workers, by principal occupational groups, within the city of Detroit in 1953 and 1965.[21]

Deskins' contribution in this area is significant because it measured changes occurring in the journey-to-work patterns of both blacks and whites by occupational group, as a function of changes in the spatial location in the residential centroid and workplace centroid for both groups respectively (Figure 3.4). In each of the previously mentioned studies a slightly different approach was employed in analyzing the problem. The results show that the distance between the place of residence of black workers and places of employment have been extended over time. The following statement extracted from Deskins' analysis sheds light on the nature of the problem:[22]

> In 1953 the majority of the metropolitan work opportunities were located in the central city. This situation generated interaction patterns which resulted in the vast majority of white workers traveling from their residential location near the city limits or in the suburbs to the central city. In the case of Negroes, their residential location, due to residential segregation, was confined to the inner city, which was also the central location for most of the metropolitan area's work opportunities. Consequently, Negro interaction between residence and work place covered comparatively shorter distances than white interaction.
>
> In twelve years the residential situation of Negroes shows little change; however shifts in work location are quite discernible.
>
> Over the years the mean distance between the residential location of black workers and work place zone has increased placing the black worker at a further disadvantage.

[20] John F. Kain, "Housing Segregation, Negro Employment, and Metropolitan Decentralization," *Quarterly Journal of Economics,* May, 1968, p. 176.

[21] Donald R. Deskins, Jr., "Interaction Patterns and the Spatial Form of the Ghetto," Special Publication No. 3, Department of Geography, Northwestern University, Evanston, Ill., 1969, p. 16.

[22] *Ibid.*

Figure 3.4 Changes in workplace and place of residence centroids in Detroit, 1953 and 1965. (Source: After Donald R. Deskins, Jr., "Interaction Patterns and the Spatial Form of the Ghetto," Special Publication No. 3, Department of Geography, Northwestern University, 1969)

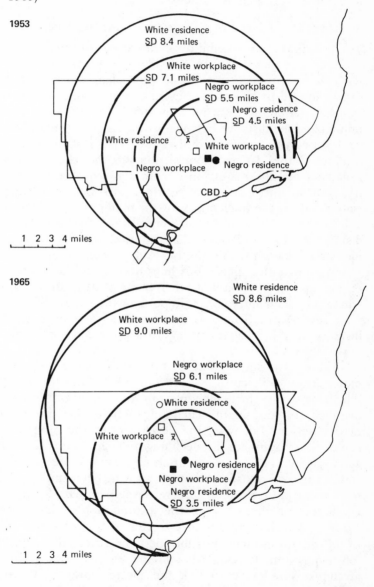

There is evidence that geographers are beginning to give increasing attention to this problem. If this apparent interest is maintained and promoted, one should be able to make more definitive statements about the extent and severity of the problem as it exists over a large number of places. While the view that the problem exists seems to be unanimous, some of the discrepancies noted in the observed severity of the problem may well represent methodological weaknesses in the problem treatment.

Strategies Designed to Overcome the Workplace Distance Effect

The principal strategy employed to date in an attempt to ameliorate the problem has been to provide transport access to suburban workplace zones. As the low-income black worker has been most disadvantaged by this turn of events, some form of public transportation has frequently been recommended and promoted as a means of minimizing the distance between worker and workplace. Intervention in this area was accelerated after the Watts riot of 1965. One of the findings of the McCone Commission was that the Watts worker was isolated from the major job growth zones by transport inaccessibility. But in the year prior to the Watts outburst, Singelton had elaborated on the inadequacy of the public transportation system to deliver the residents of South Central Los Angeles to the diverse and distant employment sites that typified the emerging pattern of industrial location within the Los Angeles metropolitan area.[2 3]

In a few cities special bus lines have been placed into operation, on an experimental basis, to deliver the ghetto worker to those areas where job availability exists. Reports of the impact of these attempts have come forth from Los Angeles, Boston, and St. Louis. In each instance this particular strategy has produced something less than hoped for results.

There have been reported difficulties in the area of bus scheduling. These difficulties grow out of failure to coordinate bus schedules with shift schedules in the zone of destination. The inability to coordinate scheduling activity has produced worker dissatisfaction. Likewise, the developers of the program have indicated disappointment in declining ridership after brief periods of employment. The latter condition frequently represents the workers' shift to private transportation after having been employed for several pay periods. In St. Louis there developed a problem of retaining employees on the job after the introduction of the transportation strategy. This has led one investigator to comment that the problem of job retention might possibly be more severe than the problem of job acquisition. It seems that in the few experimental cases where attempts were made to link the ghetto worker with employment

2 3 Robert Singelton, "Unemployment and Public Transportation in Los Angeles," *Hard-core Unemployment and Poverty in Los Angeles,* U.S. Department of Commerce, Area Redevelopment Administration, 1965.

zones, through the development of public transportation, the result was failure. There are those who contend the failure is in large measure associated with the principal mode of transportation employed—the bus.

Given the weakness of the bus as a means of enhancing the low-income ghetto workers' employment opportunities, private transportation sources have been recommended as an alternative. Myers has suggested cars for the poor which might be supported by public subsidy. It has been stated that inexpensive foreign cars would provide greater transport flexibility and reliability than the current modes of transportation available. Many employers attribute absenteeism and tardiness of ghetto employees to unreliable transportation modes. While a large percentage of inner-city residents own automobiles, many of the cars owned by the low-income segment of that population are rapidly becoming vintage models. The unreliability of these automobiles is voiced by the following statement uttered by an unknown ghetto resident: "Many ghetto residents have cars, but few have rides." Though Myer's recommendation of "New Volks for poof folks" has some merit, it is highly unlikely to receive support given the general public's notion of what constitutes adequate and appropriate transportation for the poor.[24] Alternative uses of private carriers have been suggested, but many barriers tend to exist which would make the private carrier unacceptable. While the new Volks idea may appear to be a preposterous one, a recent news photo shows waste—the destruction of a number of Japanese-built automobiles in Portland, Oregon, because of a defective heating and defrosting mechanism coupled with the inability to secure these from the distributor service outlet—which seems equally preposterous. The new Volks idea or some modification of it, while appearing to be a radical one, no doubt should be carefully scrutinized.

Finally, it appears that the problem of juxtaposing worker with workplace is not simply a mechanical one of being able to transport people over space. The attitude of some low-income black workers mitigates against the possibility of seeking out employment in what is perceived of as a hostile territory. Kalacheck and Goering report one respondent's views on the possibility of employment in St. Louis county as follows:[25] "I'm not for going out in the county, 'cause out in the county people are too different from me, you know they ain't my bag."

[24] Sumner Myers, "Personal Transportation for the Poor," *Traffic Quarterly*, April, 1970, pp. 194-203.
[25] Edward D. Kalacheck and John M. Goering, eds., *Transportation and Central City Unemployment*, Washington University, St. Louis, Mo., Mar., 1970, p. F-39.

While the attitude expressed above no doubt represents a minority point of view, it does constitute a very real problem in some areas. Such attitudes tend more often to represent the perspective of young single males with limited skills and a strong attachment to the ghetto as a place. This attitude is similar to that of segments of the white population who view their territory as inviolate. Thus the experiences of some ghetto youth mitigate against their being willing to venture far from the safety of their own refuge. In the final analysis, programs designed to overcome such fears must be promoted, as indeed they are in many programs designed to minimize the problems of the hard-core unemployed.

An altered distribution pattern of black residential households is surely the most effective way of simply overcoming the distance effect of the workplace-residence syndrome, although opposition to black suburbanization is still high. But as previously mentioned, there is growing evidence of increased black suburbanization, especially around a number of first-generation ghetto centers.[26]   Aside from the question of the nature of the communities of residence, it is apparent that this segment of the black population has removed one barrier between themselves and jobs.

The increasing polarization of the races might well work against the effectiveness of the latter strategy. There is much evidence which indicates that the government's low-income, scattered-sites housing program has encountered untold difficulty when attempts were made to select sites outside of the existing ghetto context. But continued efforts are yet in order. When we consider the enhanced employment opportunities of that segment of the black population that chose to abandon the ghettos in San Francisco and Oakland for East Palo Alto, a small residential community located 20 to 25 miles south of this central-city complex, then it becomes quite clear that the latter strategy must be pursued along with a host of others if black populations are to experience any meaningful change in their search for economic security.

THE GHETTO RETAIL ENVIRONMENT

The resident ghetto population has certain basic commercial needs, many of which might be satisfied by shopping within that territory identified as the ghetto. The question which logically comes to mind is how adequate are the retail outlets in ghetto areas in terms of satisfying the retail needs of the population residing therein. While there is no simple or singular answer to that question, there does exist a good deal of variation in the income level of local black

[26] Reynolds Farley, "Changing Distribution of Negroes within Metropolitan Areas: The Emergence of Black Suburbs," *American Journal of Sociology*, Jan., 1970, pp. 512-529.

populations, and consequently, in the response of the business sector to these differences. Although differences in retail adequacy and retail character vary spatially within the ghetto, it is thought by some that ghetto retail establishments possess a unique set of characteristics, whether measured in terms of the external appearance of the retail outlet or the internal mix of the commodity structure.

Geographers have almost totally confined their interest to the external appearance, yet the combination of the two is thought by some writers to represent the impact of black culture. Pred questioned the role of culture on the physical appearance of retail outlets, as well as the modal retail structure in areas serving a predominantly black clientele, and posited that many of these conditions might simply be associated with stores serving low-income populations.[27] But, on examining the retail structure in a low-income black residential area in Chicago, he conceded that it was possible to extract from that set of stores those which were essentially common to all low-income areas and those which were uniquely Negro in character.[28] While this argument has not been completely resolved, it is logical that subcultural differences would affect the taste of a set of consumers and that businessmen would respond to this recognized pattern in the promotion of product lines and the provision of services.

The major shortcoming of these findings is that they only describe the retail character in low-income black areas on the one hand and neighborhood-level retail centers on the other. A market analyst recently reported that the black community should not be viewed as a monolithic community, but should more appropriately be viewed segmentally as a means of improving the payoffs from advertising efforts focused on the black population.[29] This strategy has not been employed by those investigators concerned with the prevailing retail structure in ghetto areas—probably a reflection of the paucity of such research efforts and the fact that most studies have either concentrated on a single retail complex or have been so general as to ignore these kinds of differences.

In our previous discussion of ghetto business, it was acknowledged that such businesses are most often retail in character. Nevertheless, the proportion of all ghetto retail outlets owned by segments of the black population is small in number. A recent survey demonstrated that, even in New York's Harlem, 63 percent of all business is

[27] Allan Pred, "Business Thoroughfares as Expressions of Urban Negro Culture," *Economic Geography*, July, 1963, pp. 217-218.

[28] *Ibid.*, pp. 221-227.

[29] Dorothy Cohen, "Advertising and the Black Community," *Journal of Marketing*, Oct., 1970, pp. 8-9.

owned by whites.[30] The extent to which black ownership prevails is likely to differ significantly, depending upon the location of a given retail complex in the retail hierarchical structure. The more widespread black ownership of individual retail outlets is likely to be found in neighborhood centers, while the small shopping-goods centers are likely to be dominated by white-operated enterprises. The latter situation in part reflects the effect of a corporate structure and the fact that goods distributor outlets require a greater financial investment in their operation than do service outlets, which tend to be dominated by black ownership.

Blacks tend to dominate in the ownership of those businesses often called "Negro-type businesses." Usually this set of establishments engages in providing services almost exclusively to members of the group. They include barbershops, beauty shops, dry cleaning establishments, eating and drinking establishments, and record shops. The recent rise in franchised dealerships has increased the black businessman's potential for commercial involvement and, at the same time, has enhanced his opportunities to provide service within a physically attractive internal environment.

NEGRO-TYPE BUSINESSES AND GHETTO RETAIL STRUCTURE

A sizable share of all retail outlets in ghetto neighborhood centers are Negro-type businesses. The neighborhood center situated along a stretch of E. Madison Street in Seattle's black ghetto in 1965 included 10 such functions among a total of 27 retail outlets found in the center (Figure 3.5). This particular center is a small but stable one, not having been characterized by radical changes in the retail structure nor retail ownership over a 10-year period. In Milwaukee, where the territorial expanse of the black ghetto has been characterized by rapid growth, the number of Negro-type businesses situated along the various commercial thoroughfares has rapidly increased (Figure 3.6). Areas A and B shown in Figure 3.6 were heavily Negro in 1967 and were characterized by a higher density of Negro-type businesses than area C whose black population was very much smaller than that in the other zones. The proliferation of Negro-type businesses within the ghetto is a strong indication that a small but growing number of blacks are interested in trying their hand in the entrepreneurial game of chance. What is equally apparent is that the type and nature of businesses that they have chosen to enter will only enable them to become marginal capitalists, at best. Limited investment capital and lack of management experience does not

[30] Gary S. Goodpaster, "An Introduction to the Community Development Corporation," *Journal of Urban Law*, Vol. 46, Issue 3, 1968, p. 639.

Figure 3.5   The dominance of Negro-type businesses in Seattle's East Madison
Street retail nucleation, 1965.

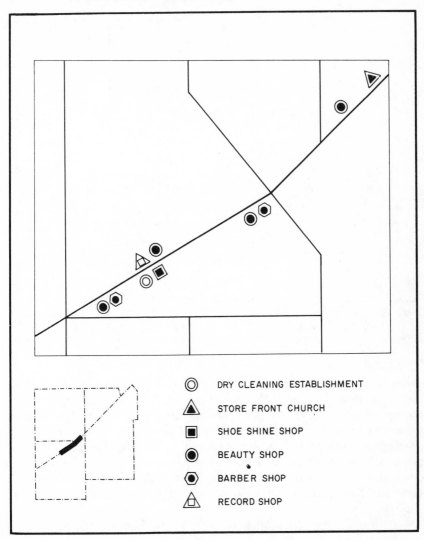

provide the black entrepreneur much leverage in the highly competitive world of business.

A few bright spots are beginning to appear, as blacks are found in
commercial operations which represent a break with the past. At
long last a few blacks have managed to acquire a limited number of
new automobile dealerships in a few of the nation's largest ghettos.
But it will continue to be difficult for blacks to gain a foothold in

Figure 3.6   The distribution of Negro-type businesses in a segment of the Milwaukee ghetto, 1967.

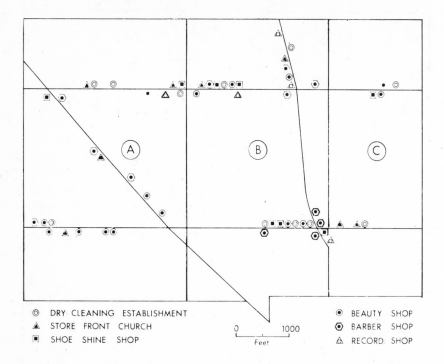

◎	DRY CLEANING ESTABLISHMENT	⦿ BEAUTY SHOP
▲	STORE FRONT CHURCH	◉ BARBER SHOP
▣	SHOE SHINE SHOP	△ RECORD SHOP

0 ____ 1000
Feet

other than neighborhood-type business enterprises, given limited investment capital and the necessity of having to compete with corporate enterprises for the more favorable locations. It is only when corporate enterprises write off a strip commercial area that it is possible for blacks to acquire the kind of facility that possesses the potential for housing a highly profitable organization. But when corporate action of this type is undertaken, the potential has generally disappeared and another slum business district has begun to emerge.

Seldom is the black business man found beyond the margins of the ghetto, a factor which tends to place restrictions on the nature of the enterprise which might be developed and further promotes the proliferation of Negro-type businesses. Black business development is essentially contingent upon the territorial expansion of black populations. As the ghetto grows so does the potential for blacks to enter business. Business streets situated in the wake of the expanding ghetto are often characterized by a transformation of their commercial structure, with the advent of a sizable number of blacks into the market area.

Race and the Dynamics of Retail Change

A neighborhood-level retail center which previously reflected the taste of a particular social group in terms of its retail mix has that mix altered as the proportion of blacks in the population increases. Not only do businesses which attempt to capture the market potential of the new population come into existence, but increasingly one witnesses the introduction into commercial structures of service agencies, which have evolved to tend the social needs of the poor. So as lower to middle-income white neighborhoods become lower to working-class black neighborhoods, the number of retail outlets serving the area tend to decline. But even more obvious is the fact that a number of outlets which previously provided a commercial service now provide a social service. Were it not for the numerous social welfare programs which came into existence during the sixties, the vacancy rate in small shopping-goods centers and community-level retail centers would be raised beyond existing levels. Commercial outlets such as banks, which were designed to provide a unique service, would have found it difficult to adapt to an alternative use had it not been for the demands created by the swift rise in the number of social service outlets during the recent past. Even so, a number of structures of this type remain empty in ghetto areas and only stand in testament to the range of services provided in the ghetto during a previous period.

As neighborhood after neighborhood undergoes changes in its racial composition, attendant changes take place in the retail structure of neighborhood retail centers and eventually of community-level and smaller shopping-goods centers. The larger and more diverse shopping-goods centers are able to stave off change for a longer period of time than the lower-level centers. In the process of change, community-level centers become neighborhood centers, and small shopping-goods centers tend to become blighted community-level centers.

The death knell to continued viability of shopping-goods centers is struck when the major department store in the complex closes its doors for a more attractive alternative location. When this occurs, the local population must travel a greater distance to secure basic commercial items that were previously available within a shorter travel radius. Within the Milwaukee ghetto there are two older shopping-goods centers. In 1963 they were characterized by comparable sales volumes, approximately 25 million dollars, although the center in what was the core of the ghetto contained the larger number of stores during this period. By 1967, the retail shopping district in the older core area had suffered both a relative and absolute loss in income, as well as a 17 percent decline in the number of stores over the four-year period. The major proportion of the decline in the number of stores was associated with the loss of shopping-goods stores.

Blight has completely engulfed the latter area and is advancing in the former. The rise of outlying shopping districts and the reduction of housing in the former trade area, through freeway development and other forms of demolition, is hastening the demise of the former, and it will not be able to survive unless extraordinary efforts are made to hold the line. Thus as the black population expands over space, there is frequently a decline in the viability of retail nucleations and subsequently the population is poorly served by locally based commercial outlets.

In many low-income ghetto areas, food outlets are dominated by the small independent operators whose operating costs are high; thus, he makes adjustments in his price structure in order to defray these and other operating costs. Cohen reports that the newer larger supermarkets have avoided low-income areas in Detroit.[31] This situation has been more extensively detailed by Sengstock, who explains that the corporate supermarkets are a white, middle-class phenomenon, thus accounting for their limited representation in low-income ghetto areas.[32] Thus, in those parts of the ghetto characterized by the lowest income levels, food, which generally represents the single largest item in the budget, is conveniently offered only at the small independent stores. The absence of stores which provide competitive pricing has resulted in recommendations that large supermarkets be encouraged to locate in such areas, especially if this action might be facilitated through existing urban renewal projects. Somewhat paradoxically it was found that discount grocers, even to a greater extent than others, tended to shun low-income black areas in Detroit.[33]

Blacks are not unaware of price differences prevailing within stores to which they have reasonable access. Goodman recently demonstrated that the black perceptions of price differences among a selected set of stores which included large supermarkets, medium-sized independents, and small stores in a low-income district in Philadelphia were reasonably accurate.[34] It was learned from this survey that prices represented the single most important determinant

[31] Saul B. Cohen, "Form and Function in the Geography of Retailing," *Economic Geography*, Jan., 1967, p. 39.

[32] Mary C. Sengstock, "The Corporation and the Ghetto: An Analysis of the Effects of Corporate Retail Grocery Sales on Ghetto Life," *Journal of Urban Law*, Vol. 45, 1968, pp. 689-690.

[33] *Ibid.*, p. 683.

[34] Charles S. Goodman, "Do the Poor Pay More?", *Journal of Marketing*, Jan., 1968, pp. 22-23.

in store choice, with quality second and distance traveled representing a poor third. So low-income black residents devise strategies that enable them to secure the best food bargains within a critical travel range. In the Philadelphia case the best bargains consistently were to be found among the medium-sized independents.[35] This is somewhat surprising in the light of the fact that there were a number of supermarkets operating in the general area. Supermarkets are sometimes accused of engaging in price zoning, a practice which permits them to lower their prices in zones of intense market competition and raise them on selected items in zones of limited competition.

It is obvious that low-income areas are not zones of intense price competition among food distributors; nevertheless the allegation of zone pricing has not been substantiated as representing a common practice. As a number of supermarkets abandon their ghetto store locations, black business groups are beginning to acquire such facilities as a means of filling the void and at the same time permitting blacks to become involved in nonmarginal commercial operations.

The question of price structure prevailing within ghetto stores in general has prompted a number of investigations during the past several years. These investigations have usually focused on price differences for common items in selected ghetto stores. Food and household appliance outlets have most often represented the type enterprises investigated. The findings have generally been inconclusive, reflecting differences in research procedures and often a lack of comparable products in the dichotomous store set. The latter situation largely characterizes the investigative problems among appliance outlets. With regard to food stores, it has been shown that different results might come from a market-basket analysis versus an itemized-listing analysis. Whether or not significant differences exist among areas in their pricing practices, it is obvious that ghetto residents perceive that such differences exist, a phenomenon which consequently affects the resident-business operator interaction pattern.

It is common knowledge that during the recent widespread wave of violence in American cities, the ghetto merchant was hardest hit. Sturdivant reports that in Los Angeles more than 95 percent of all buildings damaged by burning and looting were retail outlets.[36] Thus, alleged customer dissatisfaction with ghetto merchants is partially responsible for these stores being selected for abuse. The total question is much more complex than this and requires a more

35 *Ibid.*, p. 22.
36 Frederick D. Sturdivant, "Better Deal for Ghetto Shoppers," *Harvard Business Review*, Mar.-Apr., 1968, p. 131.

thorough analysis. Merchants in responding to the physical damage to stores during this period of widespread aggression against property either chose to modify the physical design of the facility or to abandon the area all together (Figure 3.7). The nature of the

Figure 3.7   These boarded-up structures are located on Minneapolis' Plymouth
            Street. Plymouth Street was hit hard by rampaging groups during
            a 1967 racial conflagration. Many of the former operators, includ-
            ing Knox Food Market, have indicated that they do not plan to re-
            open. Sights like this are becoming commonplace on business streets
            situated in the ghetto.

interaction pattern emerging between ghetto residents and commercial operators is beginning to produce changes in the nature of ghetto retail activity. At this point it is unclear who will emerge victorious, yet one should not be unaware that built-in deficiencies in the way the commercial system operates could in the long run result in both parties being the losers.

Most retail nucleations serving a predominantly black population are string street configurations. Since many of these string street type commercial areas are located in the more congested parts of cities, they are suffering in their attempt to compete with the evolving planned shopping centers with their spacious parking facilities and generally attractive shopping environment. Among big cities, Denver is one of the few in which retail nucleations serving the black population are not of the commercial ribbon type, at least at the neighborhood or community level. Denver, a newer city, has within the black community two small planned shopping centers. Nevertheless, Negro-type businesses are commonplace within these centers, although the appearance of the centers is far superior to that usually associated with string street developments (Figure 3.8). In East Palo

Figure 3.8 Negro-type businesses are much in evidence in Denver's Park Hill
shopping district, but they are situated in a far more attractive
physical environment than characterizes their traditional location
in string street developments.

Alto, an outlying suburban community which has been transformed into essentially a black residential community, a new shopping complex was recently completed. The annual retail spending in this community is comparable in level to that in the older small shopping-goods centers in Milwaukee. The East Palo Alto complex might be described as a community-level shopping nucleation with a smaller proportion of Negro-type businesses than is usually encountered in such centers. Black pride is overtly manifested in the external decor of the center (Figure 3.9).

CONCLUSIONS

The economic characteristics of the place-based spatial configuration loosely identified as the ghetto are associated with the level and character of employment opportunities available to its residents, the extent to which the forces of economic production found therein lend support to community development, and finally the quality of

Figure 3.9   East Palo Alto's Nairobi Village is a community-level shopping center housing 17 retail structures.

commercial services available to ghetto residents. The connection between the former and latter condition needs little detailing. There is some question as to the most appropriate direction in which the forces of economic production, operating within the ghetto context, should move to enhance their contribution to the ghetto economic state. What is certain, though, is the need for interventionist strategies which are cognizant of the impact of social forces on the workings of an economic system.

Urban economic development in the United States is largely conditioned by the opportunity to improve the profitability of the firm through the selection of sites for development which hold the highest potential for profit. The decisions which ultimately determine a specific development path are seldom totally economic, although they might purport to be. The feedback effect of these economic decisions, which are partially conditioned by social forces and often produce favorable economic equilibrium conditions in overall urban development, likewise promotes the development of islands of economic blight of which the ghetto is a prime example.

The conditions previously described represent weaknesses in the way the current economic system operates, if not in the system itself. A major overhaul in systems operation is necessary, unless it is agreed that the type of economic system that generates wide-ranging benefits for the vast majority of the nation's citizens is unable to allocate benefits in such a way as to prevent the place of residence of most black Americans from resembling that of an underdeveloped country. If the latter condition cannot be altered through the operation of the existing economic system, alternative systems will be called for. Already there is evidence that segments of the American population are willing to support the development of alternative systems for the ghetto, which differ from the system that has guaranteed economic security for most other Americans.

The inability of the existing system to function effectively in alleviating ghetto blight and the growing support for a modified ghetto economic system can only lead to continued estrangement, if the modified system fails to work. Government support for a modified socialist system within the ghetto and a capitalist system outside means certain conflict. This will be especially true if limited socialism does not appear to remedy the economic conditions in the ghetto, and full socialism is then sought exclusively for these enclaves as a last resort. Alternatively, nineteenth-century capitalism, where the small shopkeeper is the principal cog in the system, is also unable to promote ghetto economic viability. The necessity for an alternative economic system appears to be more social than economic, for any economic system that ignores the strength of social forces or at least pretends to ignore such forces is destined to fail to provide both an adequate economic and social environment for all of its citizens.

CHAPTER 4

THE GHETTO AS A FORCE IN RESHAPING URBAN AMERICA

THE CASE OF COLLECTIVE VIOLENCE

Black America's hundred-year struggle for equality of opportunity and justice before the law was culminated in the midsixties by the passage of far-reaching civil rights legislation, but also by sparks of violence aimed at ghetto gatekeepers. Although this legislative action has prompted the development of new political coalitions in the South and has fostered the appearance of blacks in the chambers of political decision-making for the first time since reconstruction, it was the fires of racial violence which did much to set the tone of urban politics in the North and West. The sit-ins and the freedom rides had done much to break down a formal legal system which openly discriminated against blacks, but these and similar techniques did not provide relief from the more subtle forms of social system oppression to be found in the urban ghettos of the North. Thus, the string of ghetto explosions, starting with the Harlem riot of 1964, set into motion a new force and new form of black protest whose long-term impact is difficult to gauge at this point.

In the more than seven years which have transpired since the onset of this new form of collective violence, thousands of lines have been written by a small army of social scientists representing a variety of disciplines and perspectives. But to date, the contribution of geographers to an understanding of this phenomenon has been minimal. Only three studies have focused on the spatial aspects of riot behavior.[1] Given the potential impact that these outbursts might have on the urban configuration, it is somewhat difficult to explain the limited interest which the discipline has displayed in this topic.

There is evidence, however, that architects are beginning to express concern over the way the urban environment might be modified to minimize the impact of criminal behavior.[2] Gold, in his recent assessment of how cities might be altered physically to rebuff the impact of criminal activity, was not specifically concerned with the question of collective violence, but it is obvious that his recommendations for altering the physical environment in such a way as to isolate the criminally prone community (the ghetto community) from the noncriminal community, by the use of physical distance or fortification, would minimize the spread of collective violence beyond the physical limits of the ghetto community. Structures within the ghetto community which have often served as the targets of ghetto anger have begun to make the necessary architectural adjustments as a means of warding off a possible siege. Thus, geographers with a strong landscape interest have foregone the opportunity to treat an aspect of culture as manifested in the adaptation of architectural forms of cultural process in most of the nation's major central cities.

RACE RIOT OR REBELLION?

The violent outbursts which have spread across the breadth of urban America during a rather brief time interval have been variously defined. Frequently they have been identified as riots, and yet many would agree that they have differed in format from the racial conflicts which characterized a previous period. Fogelson considers rioting to constitute only a single aspect of the totality of events which identify this new phenomenon.[3] On the other hand, Banfield would deny the importance of race as a precipitator of these events. Instead, the latter writer would essentially explain the occurrence of these events in terms of class-culture.[4] Banfield has developed a

1 John B. Adams and Robert Sanders, "Urban Residential Structure and the Location of Stress in Ghettos," *Earth and Mineral Sciences*, Jan., 1969, pp. 29-32; Robert C. Ming and Paul S. Salter, "A Geographic Aspect of the 1968 Miami Racial Disturbance: A Preliminary Investigation," *The Professional Geographer*, March, 1969, pp. 79-86; John B. Adams, "The Geography of Riots and Civil Disorders in the 1960's," *Economic Geography* (forthcoming), Jan., 1972.

2 Robert Gold, "Urban Violence and Contemporary Defensive Cities," *Journal of the American Institute of Planners*, May, 1970, pp. 146-159.

3 Robert M. Fogelson, "Violence and Grievances: Reflections of the 1960's Riots," *The Journal of Social Issues*, Winter, 1970, pp. 144-145.

4 Edward C. Banfield, "Rioting Mainly for Fun and Profit," in James Q. Wilson, ed., *Metropolitan Enigma*, Harvard University Press, Cambridge, Mass., 1968, pp. 284-285.

structure of behavior to explain why individuals and groups engage in the kind of activity loosely described as riotous, and none of the specified forms of behavior indicate that race, in and of itself, is a significant generator of this type of behavior. These expressions of the nature of the recently observed activity are indications, on the one hand, of its complexity, and, on the other, of how it is perceived. So, while a scholar of the stature of Banfield can claim the lack of legitimacy for behavior of this kind, based simply on racial grievances, an increasing number of blacks take the view that these are acts of rebellion designed to convince white America that a new era has arrived. While there is much room for interpretative differences in the nature and causes of riot behavior, few can deny that the events which have plagued more than 200 cities since 1964 fit into the established mold employed to define race riots. The major difference lies in the nature of the object upon which the fury has been unleashed, property. Thus, the collective violence which became the symbolic hallmark of the ghetto presence, in the 1960s was essentially associated with the destruction of property to the chants of, "Burn, baby, burn."

THE SPATIAL-TEMPORAL PATTERN OF URBAN VIOLENCE

By summer's end in 1970, seven years after the initiation of this form of violent expression, collective violence was a continuing phenomenon, although there was evidence that it had begun to wane, at least in terms of its initial form. During the early years of riot occurrence the number of outbursts during a single year were few and were initially confined to the major ghetto areas in the nation. A peak was reached in the number of annual outbursts in 1968, and since that time there has been a sharp decrease in the incidence of disorder. From a spatial perspective, the riots might be viewed as the diffusion of an innovation. The pattern of the spread of that innovation in many ways conforms to the classic patterns described in the diffusion literature. One can think of the innovation being introduced in Harlem in 1964, and a subsequent pattern of adoption spreading from this initial center. Similarly, the early adopters were represented by cities possessing sizable ghettos. Barriers to the spread of the innovation were in evidence, as the major cities of the South and the border states became late adopters. Even after an initial peak in the spread of the phenomenon had been reached in 1967 (Figure 4.1), cities with such sizable ghettos as Washington, Baltimore, St. Louis, Pittsburgh, and Gary could still be listed among nonriot cities.

The Changing Regional Pattern and Periodicity of Occurrence

Collective violence revolving around racial conflict reached its apex

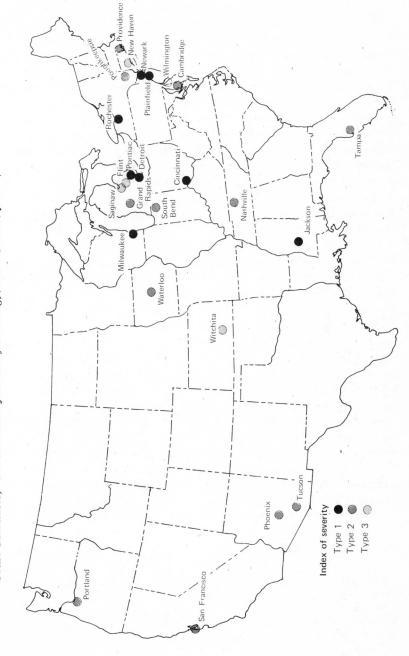

Figure 4.1 The geographic pattern of major riots, 1967. (Source: Jules J. Wanderer, "An Index of Riot Severity and Some Correlates," *The American Journal of Sociology*, March, 1969, p. 504)

in 1968, with more than 100 cities experiencing one or more outbursts. During the latter year there was an alteration in the nature of the occurrence of these events as well as a change in their spatial pattern. By the end of 1967, one had begun to think of these outbursts as essentially a summer phenomenon. But there was evidence of periodic outburst during the winter and early spring of 1968, and there was evidence as well that both high school and college students had begun to accept collective violence as a legitimate technique for resolving or addressing a variety of grievances. Thus, the technique which had evolved among Northern ghetto blacks to demonstrate dissatisfaction with their lot had now been transported to the South, where it was adopted by both black high school and college students. Drake highlights this occurrence in his description of the activity of black college students in Orangeburg, South Carolina, in protesting refusal of admission to a local white bowling alley.[5] These winter skirmishes were to lead up to the massive outbursts in April which were associated with the assassination of Dr. Martin Luther King. The King death triggered a violent reaction, and during the month of April more than 200 outbursts of violence were recorded.[6]

The year 1968 represents the turn-around year for collective violence. No longer were violent outbursts essentially confined to the major ghetto centers in the nation; they were now occurring throughout the nation, in small cities as well as large, and in Southern towns and Western cities.

By the end of the year 1968 the innovation had a universal geographic pattern of adoption. Southern cities accounted for the single largest number of violent outbursts during this period, a record which had been accorded cities in the Northeast during the previous year (Figure 4.2). Similarly, 1968 became the year during which collective violence could no longer be viewed as simply a spontaneous response to a perceived affront. Spontaneous violence was beginning to yield to planned violence as the shoot-out in Cleveland would attest.[7] Riots and the threat of riots continue to plague the nation's cities, but the number and frequency of occurrence is now smaller. The possibility, however, of occurrence in any nook and cranny of the country is an ever present reality, even though methods of bringing such behavior under control are now more effective and sophisticated.

[5] St. Clair Drake, "The Pattern of Interracial Conflict in 1968," in Pat Romero, ed., *In Black America*, United Publishing Co., Washington, D.C., 1969, p. 46.

[6] *Ibid.*, p. 42.

[7] Jeffrey K. Hadden, "Reflections on the Social Scientist's Role in Studying Civil Violence: Introduction to a Symposium," *Social Science Quarterly*, Sept., 1970, p. 220.

Figure 4.2 The geographic pattern of major riots, 1968. (Source: *Riot Data Review*, Lemberg Center for the Study of Violence, Brandeis University, Aug. 1968)

Characteristics of Riot Cities

The changing spatial pattern of the occurrence of riotous activity reduces the legitimacy of a number of studies in which objective data were employed in attempts to establish the likelihood of riot occurrence on the basis of known characteristics of place. Downes' investigation of the social characteristics of riot cities showed that riots occurred most often in cities having a high proportion of blacks in the population; rapid increase in the black population during the decade of the fifties; an absolute loss or only a minimal gain in total population during the same time interval; low level of educational attainment; lower median income; higher percentage of unsound housing; higher unemployment; low owner occupancy rate. The cities themselves were most often central-employing large central cities which were characterized by employment dominance in the following categories—manufacturing, diversified manufacturing, and diversified retail.[8]

Adams recently cited the work of Mooney, who also employed objective data, but relying on a different method of analysis, observed the strength of a number of the same factors cited by Downes.[9] Mooney's factors also included a Southern syndrome, a suburban syndrome, and a highway-spending factor. Analyses of this type have been employed not only in attempts to predict the occurrence of riots, but as a means of assessing the severity of riots. Assessments of riots and riot severity based on statistical analyses of objective data help explain the ingredients of place which tend to be associated with the occurrence of the phenomena, but do not get at the basic motivation for the occurrence of the phenomena.

The statistical analysis following the 1967 outburst indicates that the likelihood of riot behavior is smaller in Southern cities. But by the end of 1968, Southern cities were to be found more frequently among cities in which major disorders occurred than cities in any other region. The latter situation could mean that the South had simply been slow in adopting the technique of collective violence; that the strength of motivation for engaging in riot behavior revolves around the nature of the triggering incident; or that the method of reporting disorders might have affected the count.

The Nature of the Triggering Incident

It is yet unclear which of the above factors is the principal contributor to the altered regional patterns of the incidence of collective violence. It has been demonstrated that recent migrants from the South seldom participated in riots to the same extent as

[8] Bryan T. Downes, "Social Characteristics of Riot Cities," *Social Science Quarterly*, Dec., 1969, pp. 514-516.
[9] Adams, *op. cit.*

nonmigrants in cities characterized by riot experience outside of the region. Boesel attributes this pattern to regional differences in what black youth expect of society. An attempt was made to verify this point by comparing the level of self-esteem prevailing among a group of black youth in the Harlem ghetto with that the Bedford-Stuyvesant ghetto. Harlem ghetto youth, of which a much larger percentage were born in the North, were found to possess a much higher level of self-esteem than their Bedford-Stuyvesant counterpart, which included a much higher percentage of youth of Southern origin.[10] This would lead one to assume that blacks of recent Southern origin would be less likely to engage in riot behavior than youth who were native to the area.

When one considers that the triggering incident has most often involved conflict between ghetto residents and the police, it then becomes more understandable why this phenomenon was not commonplace in the South during earlier years. The lack of restraint of Southern policemen in dealing with black citizens generally would tend to promote the adoption of a different style of coping behavior, in adjusting to police practices, than that adopted outside the region. This is evidenced by the passive techniques employed by civil rights activists in their confrontations with police in cities throughout the South during the early sixties. Thus, it appears that a different type of triggering incident was necessary to prompt an initiation of widespread outburst of collective violence on the part of young Southern blacks.

The death of Martin Luther King served as a triggering mechanism of sufficient strength to promote the adoption of a technique that had previously found limited use in the South. It might at first glance appear somewhat paradoxical that Southern blacks would respond so violently on hearing of the death of the one black leader who was totally commited to a philosophy of nonviolence. But even in the Banfieldian sense this might be considered an outburst of righteous indignation, transcending the necessity for the occurrence of some local incident which might serve as the triggering incident. Thus, a number of major Southern and border cities which had not previously been the site of overt racial conflagrations could now be added to the list. The most widespread riot damage occurring during 1968 was to be found in Chicago, Washington, and Baltimore. The latter two cities, which are culturally a part of the South, were added to the list of riot cities for the first time.

There exists the possibility that the number of incidents of racial violence in the South during 1968 might have been blown out of proportion, as any incident which violated a previous pattern of

10 David Boesel, "The Liberal Society, Black Youths, and Ghetto Riots," *Psychiatry,* May, 1970, p. 268.

Southern custom might have been reported as representing a riot. Likewise, major riots, which are often defined in terms of their length or prevalence and the force required to bring them under control, might have been exaggerated as a result of calling for more force than necessary to bring the activity under control. A case in point might be made by referring to the description of the riot situation prevailing in Gainsville, Florida, on April 6-8, 1968:[11]

> 75 persons, almost all blacks, marched to the Alachua county jail on Saturday, April 6, to demand the release of Irvin "Jack" Dawkins, a black power advocate charged last month with firebombing a white-owned business in the city's black district. The march was led by members of SLIC, the University of Florida's Afro-American Student Association and the newly formed sit-in at a memorial service for Dr. King. That night mayor-commissioner Ted. E. Wilhams ordered a curfew following fire bombings and sniper fire at police. Later the same night 130 Guardsmen arrived to quell a 4 hour disturbance in the black district involving the breaking of windows of several stores and 15 car windows, small fires and some sniper fire. Guardsmen supplemented by state highway patrol troopers, campus police and a 30-man state "conservation riot squad" from a total of 366 officers at the peak of the activity.

THE MAJOR RIOTS

The number of major riots in 1968 was only about one-half the number occurring during the previous year, even though the absolute number of riots reported was greater during the latter year. Major riots in this instance are defined as those in which there was evidence of looting, arson, sniping, the use of extraterritorial enforcement personnel (state police or National Guard), and finally fatalities. In this instance the index of riot severity developed by Wanderer, including scale types 1, 2, and 3, was used to identify places where major riots occurred.[12] These scale types include places where each of the above acts of collective violence occurred in combination and it was subsequently necessary to call for military or state police reinforcements.

During 1967, 26 cities could be characterized as having major outbursts of collective violence; of these outbursts five occurred in Southern cities (see Figure 4.1). Employing data from the Lemberg

[11] Lemberg Center for the Study of Violence, *Riot Data Review,* Brandeis University, Waltham, Mass., Aug., 1968, p. 31.

[12] Jules Wanderer, "An Index of Riot Severity and Some Correlates," *The American Journal of Sociology,* Mar., 1969, pp. 503-504.

Center for the Study of Violence, an attempt was made to identify those places which in 1968 possessed violence characteristics of the same level of severity as represented by Wanderer's scale types, identified here as constituting major riots. It was found that only 13 cities could be described as having a major riot in the latter year; 7 of these were Southern cities (see Figure 4.2). Thus, by 1968 major riots were on the wane, even though the total number of incidents described as riots reached a peak during that year.

Southern cities, initially reluctant to join the column of places in which collective violence had become the order of the day, were by 1968 places of the most frequent eruption of riot behavior. This latter pattern of behavior indicates that five years were required for a technique, which was adopted initially in the Northeast, to develop a national pattern of adoption. Collective violence of the type described here, like the sit-ins, represents a regional-specific technique designed to cope with problems with which blacks were confronted under quite different sets of circumstances. On the other hand, the sit-ins, which were specifically designed to deal with a Southern phenomenon, overt segregation, later spread to places outside of the South where their success was questionable. Collective violence essentially represented an attempt to cope with problems of covert discrimination of the type which prevails outside of the South, but was later to transcend the boundaries of its region of origin. One is unable to state with certainty if a phenomenon, which alerted public officials and private citizens alike that all was not well in the ghettos of the North and West, had the same effect on public officials in Southern cities. Some are of the opinion that its chief effect was that of promoting a national coalition, which allowed Southerners to provide widespread support to the Republican party, but at the same time permitted George Wallace to make greater political inroads outside the South.

THE GEOGRAPHY OF GHETTO RIOTS

While it is appropriate to discuss riot cities and the objective characteristics of those places in which such events occur, most of the events were confined to a very limited area within the cities in which they occurred. Acts of collective violence have been essentially confined to locations within the ghetto community (Figure 4.3), although there is evidence that people residing outside of the ghetto are fearful of the spillover effects of riots or that blacks will attempt to stage attacks beyond the limits of their perceived turf. The heightened activity associated with gun purchases by suburban and nonsuburban residents alike, immediately following outbreaks of violence, reflects these fears.

Figure 4.3 Ghetto neighborhood types within the Detroit riot zone.

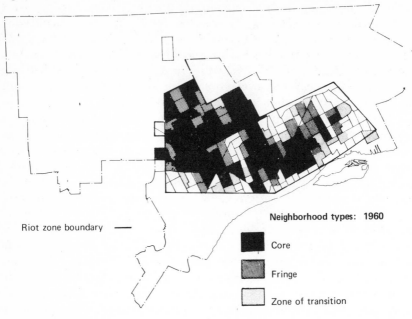

Riot zone boundary ——

Neighborhood types: 1960

■ Core

▨ Fringe

☐ Zone of transition

Riot Causation

In attempting to assess the cause of riots, one must look to the environment in which they occur and the kind of black/white interaction patterns that take place within that environment. To some, ghetto riots are seen as outbursts of suppressed rage.[13] Poussaint states that this rage is directed at those whom ghetto residents view as the oppressors—store owners and policemen.[14] The white population with whom most ghetto residents have contact or observe within the ghetto territorial configuration are policemen and retail merchants. Increasingly, the police have been viewed as occupying armies, while merchants are often seen as exploiters. Antagonism between police, merchants, and ghetto residents has been building up for some time; thus both the insiders and outsiders view one another with suspicion and mutual distrust. A relationship such as this can only be expected to terminate in outbursts of violence.

[13] Alvin F. Poussaint, "The Psychology of a Minority Group with Implications for Social Action," in Charles U. Daly, ed., *Urban Violence,* University of Chicago Center for Policy Study, 1969, pp. 32-33.
[14] *Ibid.,* p. 33.

It is generally conceded that the perceptions held by residents of the ghetto relative to their position in society is the key to urban unrest. In attempting to explain the causes of riots, the relative deprivation theory appears the most satisfactory, at least in terms of the results gleaned from survey data which were collected following the riots. A survey conducted in the Detroit riot neighborhood several weeks following that outburst demonstrated that the majority of the persons interviewed felt relatively deprived in terms of their goal orientations and actual accomplishments.[15] Persons who were identified as relatively gratified, it was shown, were less likely to support riot behavior as a vehicle for promoting the groups's cause. Surprisingly, or not so surprisingly, support for riot behavior has been recorded as receiving the backing of one-third to one-half of ghetto residents in a number of cities in which major riots have occurred.[16] Thus, while riot participation rates are found to be much lower than this, support for riots as an appropriate form of behavior vis-à-vis the ghetto resident's perception of the environment in which he spends most of his life has more support than many would expect.

There is evidence of some selectivity among the ghetto population which supports riot behavior as an appropriate form of behavior. Riot supporters are more likely to be youthful males, who are natives rather than migrants and who find themselves on the margin of the job market. The greatest support for riot behavior is associated with that segment of the black population which is 16 to 25 years of age. This also happens to coincide with the age group which has the highest level of unemployment among ghetto residents. Flaming found that the greatest dissatisfaction prevailing among blacks who had been arrested during the Milwaukee riots was the absence of adequate job opportunities.[17] In most of the cities which have had major riots the level of unemployment has been higher for rioters than nonrioters. As a matter of fact, there is strong resemblance between the level of unemployment between riot participants and the young black male populations in general. This latter condition has prompted some writers to view blocked opportunities as the principal cause of riots.

Frequently, however, riots are viewed by nonghetto residents as reflecting the inadequacies of individual personalities, the lack of

15 Thomas J. Crawford and Murray Naditch, "Relative Deprivations, Powerlessness, and Militancy: The Psychology of Social Protest," *Psychiatry*, May, 1970, pp. 210-212.

16 Nathan Caplan, "The New Ghetto Man: A Review of Recent Empirical Studies," *Journal of Social Issues*, Vol. 26, No. 1, 1970, p. 60.

17 Karl H. Flaming, "Who Riots and Why? Black and White Perspectives in Milwaukee," mimeographed, Milwaukee Urban League, Oct., 1967, p. 27.

effective black leadership, the work of outside agitators, a communist plot, and a number of other conditions which tend to place the emphasis for such behavior on human inadequacy rather than on the weaknesses of the system. The gap between white and black perceptions of the causes for riot behavior and the consequences of riot behavior is wide indeed, a situation which is understandable since the two groups have arrived at their assessments from a different social, economic, political, and psychological vantage point. Until there is a greater convergence between objective conditions of black and white Americans, subjective views will cause blacks to consider riot behavior an acceptable tool to be employed by ghetto youth and whites to look upon riots as a despised tactic which must be brought under control at any cost. The latter situation becomes even more difficult as riot behavior takes on the meaning of a political ideology, as there is growing evidence that it has. There seems to be a movement away from this form of behavior, as a kind of spontaneous reaction to a prevailing set of conditions, to an organized movement designed to alter a social system which breeds the kind of conditions that one previously reacted to in an unorganized fashion. Needless to say, this new direction is at least partially attributable to the enormous gap which prevails among ghetto and nonghetto residents in their perception of objective conditions prevailing in American society in general and in the ghetto in particular.

The Riot Area

The riot area in the ghetto tends to vary from city to city depending upon the location of the incident which served as the triggering mechanism. Most often the triggering mechanism has been associated with some incident which involved the police and ghetto residents. Therefore sites having a high probability for serving as the jump-off point for riots are places around which large numbers of persons gather to engage in social discourse. It is common knowledge that much social interaction between blacks takes place on the street, and frequently a favorite street-corner hangout evolves, with easy access to a set of taverns, pool halls, or other meeting places, which tends to periodically intensify the density of a select black population. It is these areas which are under constant police surveillance and thus potential jump-off points for riot behavior given the proper ingredients. Once riotous behavior is initiated, it spreads from these jump-off points, generally along an axis which represents the string shopping street. In large cities such as Detroit, once the word is out that a riot is underway, a secondary explosion is likely to occur along an alternative commercial axis without the benefit of a triggering incident. In this instance the contagion effect is in operation.

The direct physical impact of collective violence is almost always confined to a rather limited area which generally coincides with the length of a segment of older commercial strip developments. It appears that most often the shopping areas which come under attack are low-order shopping districts, a situation which no doubt generally reflects the black entrepreneurs' inability to locate in higher order shopping areas. This indicates that commercial structures (taverns, etc.) which serve as social gathering places for blacks seldom gain a foothold in other than neighborhood districts or, if in higher order districts, it is only after they have begun the process of transformation from higher order to lower order districts.

The bulk of the damage associated with these outbursts usually represents an estimate of the loss associated with commercial structure and their inventory. Unfortunately, from the rioter's perspective, many of the commercial structures in older areas accommodate residential occupants on their upper floors. As much of the ensuing property loss is associated with arson, low-income black families suffer property losses along with those suffered by the object of the attack, the exploiting merchant. In some instances only white merchants have been victims of the torch; in others there has been no apparent selectivity in the choice of merchant to hit on the basis of race. But there is strong evidence that certain kinds of commercial operations are most often singled out for attack. In Watts, Newark, and Detroit, the principal types of businesses which came under attack were groceries, supermarkets, furniture, and liquor stores.[18] Aside from the mom-and-pop groceries, most of the businesses which have come under attack are white-owned. Black merchants in their quest for protection during such events often display evidence of black identity, such as crudely or hastily constructed signs which often only say "soul brother" (Figure 4.4).

The initial assessment of damage in riot areas was inflated as later reevaluations have shown. But, nevertheless, damage has been extensive. During the 1968 outbreaks of collective violence in Washington and Chicago, it was estimated that more than 40 percent of the businesses engaging in retail and service trade were damaged or looted.[19] Arson and looting, the hallmarks of collective violence, have taken a heavy toll on commercial structures and commercial activity in ghetto locations in which riots have occurred. It is these elements of the ghetto landscape which have served as the props on the stage on which a drama of symbolic violence has unfolded.

[18] Russell Dynes and E. L. Quarantelli, "What Looting in Civil Disturbances Really Means," *Trans-action*, May, 1968, p. 13.

[19] Howard Aldrich and Albert J. Reiss, Jr., "The Effect of Civil Disorders on Small Business in the Inner City," *Journal of Social Issues*, Vol. 26, No. 1, 1979, p. 191.

Figure 4.4 During the Milwaukee riot of 1967, hastily scrawled signs indicating
that specific shops were owned or managed by blacks were much in
evidence along the shopping strip.

Most of the arrests of persons engaged in riotous activity have
been associated with acts against property. The wholesale removal of
goods from stores has often been viewed symbolically as liberating
goods for which the customer has already paid through the charge of
excessive prices by exploiting merchants, and thus a carnival atmosphere surrounds this phase or stage in the riot drama. It is at this
point some writers have indicated that there is a redefinition of
property. Needless to say, this is not the view held by persons in the
larger metropolitan context. The impact of collective violence on the
retail structure and stability of areas having gone through a riot is
severe. In many areas the scarred and burned-out buildings take on
the appearance of a war-ravaged area (Figure 4.5). In some instances
the rubble is not cleared away perhaps as a reminder of the impact or
simply because of inefficiency in government. Increasingly, white
ghetto merchants who have not already abandoned their operations
are exhibiting evidence of their desire to leave the area. In most
instances, white abandonment has not been translated into increased
black commercial dominance, but only in the reduction of the
availability of commercial goods and services.

Figure 4.5   Fires in the Detroit ghetto, 1967. (Source: *Detroit News*)

Riot and Nonriot Neighborhoods

To date very limited attention has focused on place and its effect on riot behavior. Place in this instance refers to ghetto neighborhoods. Warren's analysis of a sample of Detroit ghetto neighborhoods represents one of the few attempts to assess the impact of neighborhood character on riot behavior. A sample of Detroit neighborhoods were surveyed, both before the occurrence of the 1967 riots and following the riots, and were later categorized on the basis of a structured neighborhood typology.[20] The neighborhood typology employed reflected the strength of the resident's identification with his neighbors and neighborhood institutions vis-à-vis the larger community.

In those neighborhoods where the local pattern of social interaction was strong, counterriot behavior prevailed during the riots; on the other hand, neighborhoods characterized by an absence of neighboring and a limited period of residence were frequently associated with riot behavior. Positive reference orientation was associated with both riot and counterriot neighborhoods, although the basis for that orientation differed. In those neighborhoods where

[20] Donald I. Warren, "Neighborhood Structure and Riot Behavior in Detroit: Some Exploratory Findings," *Social Problems,* 1969, pp. 464-470.

there was limited social interaction and weak identity structure, the tendency to withdraw in a riot situation was pronounced.

Riot neighborhoods tended to be categorized as transitory, while counterriot neighborhoods were characterized as integrated. Integration in this instance refers not to the racial composition of the neighborhood, but the extent to which residents identified with the institutions of the larger society. Another category, the diffuse neighborhood, was largely associated with the presence of a with-drawal population. While the Warren analysis has provided insight into the expected ghetto territorial response patterns during out-bursts of collective violence, public officials tend to view the ghetto essentially as a monolithic structure. For instance, during the Watts riot a curfew was imposed on the 46.5 square mile area of Los Angeles, a zone which encompassed about three-fourths of the county's black population.[21]　The Watts community occupied only a limited area within the curfew zone.

What the Detroit data show is that blacks who have been left out of the system in terms of absorbing the values of the larger society are the most bitter and are inclined to strike out at those institutions and persons who have rejected them or have hampered their opportunities for development. Those members of the black popula-tion who have encountered greater success in coping with the system tend to be identified as counterrioters. The poverty neighborhoods in which large segments of the population have abandoned hope tend to engage in withdrawal behavior. Riot behavior in Detroit was largely concentrated in working-class neighborhoods with only limited riot-ing occurring in poverty neighborhoods (Figure 4.6). The lack of an open social system has made it necessary for blacks to compete largely with one another for limited resources; the result is heighten-ed alienation between the have and have-not segments of the black population. It appears, though, that the riots have strengthened the bonds that bind ghetto residents, as there is increasing evidence of cooperation among blacks across income and social class.

WHERE WILL IT ALL END?

The riots of the sixties have not yet completely disappeared, as occasional flareups continue to occur. While the riots are abhorred by most, they have been responsible for increasing efforts to provide black people greater access to the American opportunity structure. They have likewise spurred greater surveillance by the police and have thereby created a continuing potential source of conflict. The spontaneous uprisings of only a few years ago are giving way to

[21] David O. Sears, and John B. McConahay, "Participation in the Los Angeles Riot," *Social Problems*, 1969, p. 5.

Figure 4.6 The spatial class structure within the Detroit riot zone.

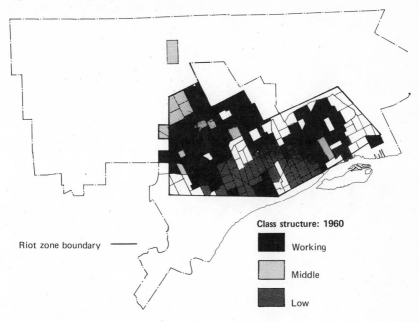

Riot zone boundary ⎯⎯⎯

Class structure: 1960

◼ Working

▨ Middle

▦ Low

organized activity in which violence against persons is beginning to assume greater importance than violence against property. The latter trend could go a long way toward transforming the nation's cities into armed camps and ultimately resulting in the evolution of urban forms which may be quite different from the traditional city.

CHAPTER 5

POLITICS AND GHETTO DELIVERY SYSTEMS

The black community has been viewed historically as a dependency that is subject exclusively to decisions made beyond its territorial realm. The absence of political input from residents indigenous to the community is well known, but attempts are actively being made to alter this situation. Unlike other major ethnic communities in this country who have used the political potential of spatial clustering to acquire advantage in securing jobs and numerous other benefits, including major inputs into the political decision-making process, blacks have remained essentially powerless even though they are more spatially segregated than any previous ethnic group in American cities. All of this is now beginning to change, but change is slow and is coming at a time when the inherited territory is one that has often been written off as possessing little opportunity for salvaging. Thus, as blacks finally begin to participate in the political life of their communities, it is at a time when political participation in the traditional sense, without major system change, could result in few gains and an increasing sense of frustration. Even though this might be the case, there is evidence that blacks have not fully given up on the possibility of transforming their communities from "communities of hope" to "communities of satisfaction," utilizing the channels that were used by previous groups in their quest for power and community control.

THE POLITICAL SYSTEM AND BLACK INVOLVEMENT

The American political and social system impinges upon the black community in such a way as to render it impotent in terms of the

102

role it plays in determining the nature and quality of services it receives, a condition which promotes disaffection as hope is abandoned. To use the jargon currently in vogue, it is found that blacks have little control over the basic delivery systems which condition social, psychological, and economic well-being. The whole delivery systems analogy grows out of a recognition for needed system change if blacks are to be the recipients of improved basic services. The systems which will be touched upon here are education, health, and safety. Others might have been chosen, but these are considered basic and are amenable to community control or at least to greater citizen involvement in determining the nature and quality of the service received. The bundles of service which are presently delivered to the black community do not produce the kind of payoffs that generate a strong black community; nor do they permit the bulk of the people to go forward and participate competitively in the larger society, and subsequently to receive the rewards associated with either personal development and/or community development which have accrued to others in American society.

Since the specified delivery systems are highly sensitive to decisions made in the political arena, it is the basic goal of this chapter to link the role of black involvement in a political system to alterations in the quality of service delivered in the ghetto subsystem with only limited inputs from the residents of that subsystem. It is the thinking of an increasing number of people that the quality and nature of services received by ghetto residents will not be appreciably changed until the recipients of the service have a greater voice in shaping the policies that directly affect them. The current holders of power have demonstrated little willingness to relinquish even a modicum of control to local residential groups, as is evidenced by the raging conflict between local governments and those promoting the concept of citizen participation which was incorporated into the major poverty legislation of the middle sixties. The question remains, How do ghetto residents make the political system more responsive to their needs? Many feel that system sensitivity will only come about through the acquisition of power. Thus the call for "black power" reflects the need to make the nation responsive to the needs of black Americans residing either within or outside the ghetto.

THE GHETTO AND THE POLITICAL SYSTEM

Black territorial communities appear to possess the political power potential necessary to transform them into environments which are conducive to healthy economic and social growth. The strength of this conviction is partially evidenced by the growing rejection on the part of black people of the idea that the ghetto as a physical entity must be destroyed. Black activists are beginning to realize that, with the continued concentration of black people in the largest central cities in the nation, black power is even more a perceived reality. There seems to be some validity associated with this position as the recent rise in the number of black elected officials attests.

The Black Proportion in the Population and the Potential for Victory

The increasing shift in the racial composition of the congressional districts in the major central cities has sent six black congressmen to the House of Representatives during the previous five years. In certain instances the creation of new districts has aided and abetted this situation. Not only have population shifts resulted in the acquisition of a small number of congressional seats, but these shifts have thrown the mayorality up for grabs in those few cities where blacks have attained a simple majority or are close to becoming the majority population.

In three of the major central cities where black candidates ran for the office of mayor and won, the black proportion in the total population exceeded 40 percent and it constituted more than half in two others. Only Carl Stokes, who possessed both charm and previous political experience as a state legislator, was able to capture the mayoral position without his city having a black majority (Figure 5.1). In both Los Angeles and Detroit, where the proportion of blacks in the population was smaller, although in the Detroit case only minimally smaller, black mayoral candidates were defeated. In Gary and Newark blacks won the top political office at that point in time when these communities were going into a state of economic stagnation and decline. But nevertheless black success is clearly attributed to the existence and growth of the ghetto.

The Territorial Scale of Intraurban Political Units and Potential for Victory

While major black spatial concentrations are commonplace throughout the nation, it is only when those concentrations develop spatial patterns that are congruent with spatial political configurations that blacks are assured of political victory. It is only in that set of small black political concentrations found outside a number of central cities that blacks have control over their residential environment. Thus, while the potential for winning political office is on the increase, it is only when blacks constitute a sizable proportion of the total population or have fostered the development of politically independent communities that this potential is transformed into reality. In either instance it appears that black officeholders have gained political advantage during the most difficult stage in the urban growth process, in those places where political victories have been won.

Figure 5.1 A black mayor's territorial support base in the Cleveland general election, 1967. (Source: Jeffrey K. Hadden, Louis H. Masott, and Victor Thiessen, "The Making of the Negro Mayors, 1967," *Transactions*, Jan.-Feb., 1968, p. 26.

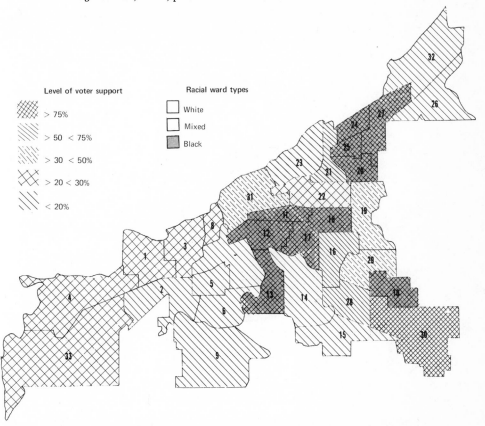

In attempting to assess the formal political power that black populations have amassed as a result of ghetto expansion, one finds that it varies in part as a function of the scale of the unit employed as the basic political subunit. Wilson, in his evaluation of black political involvement in Chicago and New York, points out that a black representative was elected to Congress at a much earlier date (1928) in Chicago than was the case in New York (1944), even though New York had a larger black population at the earlier date.[1] The small-ward system which prevails in Chicago is acknowledged to have provided the advantage which permitted blacks to succeed in being elected to political office (Figure 5.2). New York, with its large-ward system and its polynucleated pattern of ghetto development, retarded black political involvement. The small-ward system is

---

[1] James Q. Wilson, *Negro Politics*, Free Press, Glencoe, Ill., 1960, pp. 26-27.

the more efficient political organizing unit under conditions of machine politics, for it permits one to take advantage of ethnic spatial clustering by dealing with these groups in an intimate fashion at the local level. Thus the small-ward system promotes the occurrence of one type of political advantage which facilitates the possibility of being elected to political office.

Figure 5.2 Chicago's black ghetto and the small-ward system.

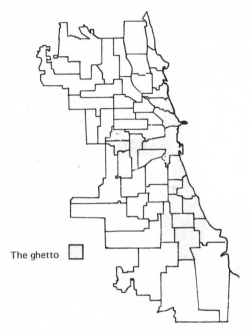

The ghetto

The political system under which this condition prevails, the machine system, may not address itself to the needs, other than selected welfare needs, of the group. The current attempt of the Reverend Jessie Jackson to challenge the supremacy of the Daley machine in Chicago reflects the perceived inability of the machine system to address itself effectively to the current and conflicting needs of individual groups.

The small-ward system does permit a large number of blacks access to the statehouse as a result of the territorial expansion of the ghetto. In 1971 both Chicago and New York had two black elected representatives in Congress, but Illinois had a larger number in the state legislature. It is in the state legislature that black political representatives can shed the shackles of machine political influence and work toward being representatives of the people. Needless to say, not all political advantage is associated with the possibility of election to political office. Blacks might be appointed to positions within the governmental structure which could place them in key decision-making roles. While Chicago succeeded much earlier than New York in getting a larger number of blacks elected to political office, New York had a better record in the area of political appointees. In the late fifties Chicago had only three black judges, at which time seventeen black judges were on the bench in New York.[2] By 1967 Chicago had moved forward in the area of judicial appointments with nine, while New York continued with seventeen.[3] Stone grants that blacks in Chicago have an edge over New York in political power, expressed through the use of his Index of Proportional Equality, although he indicates blacks have been able to secure top-level administrative posts with greater facility in New York, a factor which he attributes to the latter city's greater sophistication.[4] In those cities where local political officials are elected on an at-large basis, blacks have tended to fare poorly.

POPULATION CHANGES AND REDUCED POLITICAL POTENTIAL

The previous advantages which have accrued to the black community and more specifically to the potential black officeholder may have reached their apex in individual cities. This is no doubt less true for the post of mayor, but the process of internal population shifts within metropolitan areas and the absolute loss in central-city populations will result in the rearrangement of the boundaries of congressional districts. Under the latter condition of reorganization it is possible for districts which now include black congressmen to be gerrymandered in such a way as to result in the defeat of such congressmen. In Detroit, one of the two cities in the country with two black congressmen, the loss in population between 1960 and 1970 exceeded that of any other American city in absolute numbers. Hardest hit by this loss were congressional districts 13 and 1, districts represented by black congressmen (Figure 5.3). District 13, the stronghold of Congressman Diggs, lost almost a quarter of its population during the interval, while the second largest loss occurred in the district of Congressman Conyers. To be sure, all Detroit congressional districts lost population, but none of the magnitude of District 13. A similar situation occurred in St. Louis where there was a 19-percent decline in population in the First Congressional District of Representative William Clay. The paradox revolves around the necessity of blacks to have a majority or near majority black

[2] *Ibid.*, p. 46.
[3] Chuck Stone, *Black Political Power in America*, Bobbs-Merrill, Indianapolis, Ind., 1968, p. 361.
[4] *Ibid.*, pp. 160-162.

constituency to be elected to political office at this level, unless there exists a unique combination of circumstances such as those that permitted Representative Dellums of California to be elected from a district which was not principally black.

Figure 5.3 Population change in selected congressional districts, 1969-1970. (Source: 1970 Census of Population, PC(P3)-1, Preliminary Reports, Population of Congressional Districts)

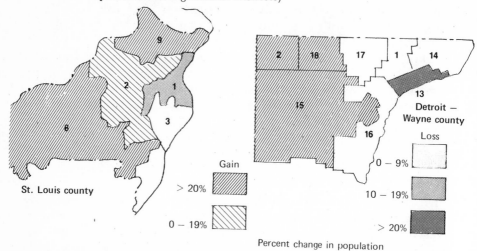

Percent change in population

Paradoxically, the absolute loss in total central-city population is occurring at the same time that there is an increase in the magnitude of the Black population in these urban centers. Detroit now has the third largest black population to be found in an American central city, but such an increase has only assured it of a possible loss of its black congressional representation pending the outcome of congressional redistricting. With the increased size of the total national population over the 10-year period, the average size of the population per congressional district should increase from approximately 410,000 to 473,000. The actual size of congressional districts tends to vary somewhat from state to state, but the population of most districts ranges from 380,000 to 440,000. If a similar or a slightly higher value for the range in size of congressional districts is employed on the basis of new census information, congressional districts will range in population from 423,000 to 523,000 persons. Congressional districts of this size will make it necessary to change the scale of the district in those central cities which were characterized by population losses in the direction of expansion. Meanwhile, numerous suburban census districts will have to be compressed to place them within the mean population range. The big question which remains is how congressional redistricting will proceed.

If we choose, for example, the existing congressional district structure of St. Louis county, then one can begin to speculate about outcomes. It is apparent that area from either or both of Districts 2 and 9 will have to be annexed to District 1 in order for it to be brought back into adjustment on the basis of population size. District 1 will require an addition of from 65,000 to 165,000 persons to place it within the new district population range. The absolute number of persons chosen to constitute the new district will have implications for the potential of supporting a black congressional candidate. Since congressional districts are based on numbers of people rather than the number of people of voting age, this could severely alter the political advantage the black candidate possesses under the presently prevailing structure. Districts 2 and 9 are overwhelmingly white growth districts, no doubt partially made up of persons who have abandoned the central city for the amenities of suburbia.

The ultimate decision on the geographic form of congressional districts will tentatively be decided in the statehouse. Fortunately, Missouri has 13 black state legislators. The Detroit situation is the more serious in terms of the prospects of loss of black political power. There exists the possibility of merger of Districts 1 and 13 as the combined population of the two was only approximately 700,000 in 1970. In this instance, since contiguous districts also lost population, reorganization might be carried out in such a way as to combine white districts with white districts and black districts with black districts. The former attempt would probably see the northern sectors of Districts 17, 1, and 14 combined, which would eliminate the white population from District 1. This would result in the merger of the truncated section of District 1 with District 13. Thus Conyers and Diggs would be left to fight for control of the newly organized district. Population redistribution apparently increases black opportunity for control of the central city, but at the same time it reduces the possibility of political representation at the national level. For those who support the concept of urban federalism, it seems that this support would be weakened by the shift of congressional power to suburban districts.

Social Class and Political Participation

The inability of blacks to become directly involved in decision-making at the local level has led increasingly to the demand for community control. As population shifts continue and the ghettos in major American cities become territorially extensive. there develops an identifiable spatial class hierarchy within the ghetto subsystem. Most ghetto residents tend to reside in low-income and working-income neighborhoods, with the smallest proportion of a city's ghetto population being found in the apex of this hypothetical spatial configuration (Figure 5.4). During the embryonic state of ghetto development, spatial class crystallization is not highly evident, because the black population within the confines of the ghetto tends to represent a rather heterogeneous group. Once the population reaches some critical size threshold, say, for instance, 25,000, then one begins to see evidence of territorial variations in the economic characteristics of its population.

Figure 5.4 A hypothetical model of the spatial class structure of the black ghetto.

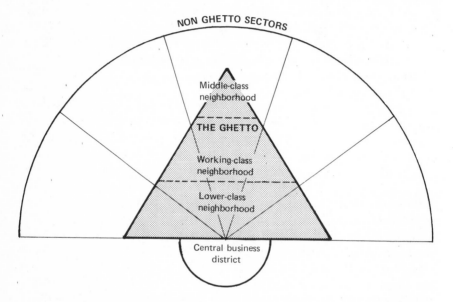

Traditionally, black political officeholders have come from the middle-class districts of the ghetto, as they represented the more articulate and better educated individuals within the community. The middle-class orientation of most elected black officials has prompted them to emphasize the first principle of legitimacy in political modernization. According to Hamilton, the first principle of legitimacy emphasizes the role of the individual and is predicated upon an egalitarian-libertarian tradition.[5] This pattern has resulted in the cooptation of black elected officials who must play by the rules established by the system of which they are a part. Since the ghetto is being increasingly viewed as a zone of economic underdevelopment within American cities, it is suggested that the second principle of legitimacy is more meaningful in altering the present ghetto situ-

[5] Charles V. Hamilton, "Conflict, Race and System-Transformation in the United States," *Journal of International Affairs*, Vol. 23, No. 1, 1969, pp. 107-108.

ation. The second principle emphasizes the role of the collectivity or group and represents the strategy most often chosen by developing nations.[6] A basic criticism of this strategy is that it is undemocratic. The implications are clear that the problems of the nation's ghettos cannot be resolved without some major alterations in the operation of the political system. Black, elected officials from middle-class backgrounds are known at times to possess basic conflicts with that group whom they represent—black, lower- and working-class populations. But under the conditions which presently exist, it is only this segment of the black population which is likely to be elected to public office. The inability of the few black elected officials and the unwillingness of white elected officials to effectively assist in the alteration and transformation of the ghetto system into an open system did much to spark the protest movement within the ghetto during the sixties.

The protest movement within big-city ghettos resulted in the rise of new organizations and new styles of leadership designed to accelerate system change. Unlike black elected officials, not all of the new protest leaders were from middle-class backgrounds nor did they all possess middle-class orientations; thus the stage was set for conflict within and outside the ghetto community. A recent study of protest leaders and black politicians in San Francisco showed that protest leaders tended to represent a much more heterogeneous lot in terms of background.[7] These leaders were locally oriented and were of the opinion that direct action would lead to attempts to ameliorate the problems of the ghetto. Black elected officials had to assume a world view, as they had to work with persons outside of the ghetto as a means of arriving at political compromise. The elected political officers tended to be a bit wary of some protest organizations, and they themselves generally only held membership in the respectable older established organizations. Hamilton recently attempted to clarify the problem of identification of black leadership styles as a means of dismissing the various dichotomous cliches which are currently being employed to describe the two types of leadership mentioned above. He recognized the following four leadership styles as operating within the ghetto:[8] (1) the political bargainer; (2) the moral crusader; (3) the alienated reformer; and (4) the alienated revolutionary.

[6] *Ibid.*, p. 109.

[7] Richard Young, "The Impact of Protest Leadership on Negro Politicians in San Francisco," *The Western Political Quarterly*, Mar., 1969, pp. 100-105.

[8] Hamilton, *op. cit.*, pp. 112-116.

The Evolution of New Leadership Styles

Most black elected officials are political bargainers by necessity and tend to be principally interested in a more equitable distribution of goods and services for their constituency. The alienated reformer, on the other hand, tends to have less faith in the existing political structure and wants not only a more equitable distribution of goods and services for ghetto residents, but also a greater role in the decision-making power. Leadership types two and four tend to represent modifications of the orientation or operation of styles one and three. Not only are class differences reflected in these leadership styles, but age is likewise a factor. This latter point was highlighted in a recent study designed to identify black leaders in the Newark ghetto. It was demonstrated that the black leaders over forty, who were employed by the government and who now were suburban residents, tended to be very traditional in their preference of civil rights groups, while those below the age of forty generally rejected the traditional civil rights groups.[9] This implies that the more activist oriented groups characterized by the leadership style of the alienated reformers are likely to gain increasing support in the ghetto community as time goes on. The recent election of a black mayor in Newark will no doubt intensify the cooperation between the political bargainer and the alienated reformer.

In black working-class and lower-class neighborhoods, new organizations and leadership styles are evolving which reflect dissatisfaction with the older organizations, perceived as having largely benefited the black middle-income populations. Thus, with spatial class filtering within the ghetto context, it becomes increasingly apparent that the first principle of political legitimacy has not led to the amelioration of the conditions of life which ghetto dwellers confront daily, but at the same time it has permitted rewards to accrue to a small proportion of the black community who are thus quite comfortable in supporting this principle. The outcome of this conflict is the current plea for community control which is increasingly heard within the black community.

Opposition to Community Control

The notion that community control be granted to resident populations within central cities has met with much opposition from a wide variety of sources. Many former liberals see this as a backward step that would lead to further racial separation and have thus accused its advocates of being separatist. Pettigrew, who understands the basis for the demands that have come from some quarters of the black community, points out that such demands are based on group pride,

---

[9] Marian Palley, Robert Russo, and Edward Scott, "Subcommunity Leadership in a Black Ghetto," *Urban Affairs Quarterly,* Mar., 1970, pp. 299-301.

but nevertheless he expresses the fear that this strategy could lead to the following condition:[10] Black separation and white separatism might well congeal to perpetuate a racially separate nation. Pettigrew is skeptical that this strategy will play into the hands of those who choose to maintain a separatist society for reasons other than those espoused by blacks, who advocate autonomy before contact. Elazar points out that a strange twist has emerged with regard to this situation, as the advocates of big government and the opponents of local control have become the conservatives.[11] These philosophical arguments aside, efforts are underway to provide local populations with a greater voice in the decision-making structures which influence the quality of life.

As America becomes more and more suburbanized, a larger share of the population does indeed have local control over their governments. Altshuler points out that small-scale government is the American norm,[12] and thus blacks are only seeking what the majority of the population already has within the territory which they currently occupy. Local control would permit persons to participate in government who would not have this opportunity under the existing structure. Such a strategy could lead to an improved image of both oneself and one's community, a condition that is highly desirable. Thus, the movement toward local community control is designed to promote participation on the part of members of the black community who have normally been excluded from the decisions which directly affect them. This recommendation has come only after all else has apparently failed—as the institutions which previously operated within the territory currently occupied by blacks fail to respond to the needs of the new population. To date, most efforts at community control have been experimental at best. It is the objective of the remainder of this chapter to view the failure of three basic community institutions and the recommendations for altering the effectiveness of these institutions by transferring greater control over them to the populations which they serve.

THE GHETTO EDUCATIONAL SYSTEM

Inner-city shcools have had only limited success in preparing black youth to fill productive niches in American society. It is frequently alleged that the schools push out those who have

---

[10] Thomas F. Pettigrew, "Racially Separate or Together?", *Journal of Social Issues*, Vol. 25, No. 1, 1969, p. 46.

[11] Daniel J. Elazar, "The Outlook for Creative Federalism," in Roland L. Warren, ed., *Politics and the Ghettos*, Atherton Press, New York, 1969, pp. 104-105.

[12] Alan A. Altshuler, *Community Control*, Pegasus, New York, 1970, p. 26.

potential and fail altogether in dealing with those who have only limited potential. Black parents have become increasingly dissatisfied with the nature of the preparation that their children are receiving and are beginning to demand some kind of accountability from those whom they hold responsible for providing education.

BLACK INVOLVEMENT IN GHETTO EDUCATION

In the past, blacks have had little control over the educational process as they have usually been absent in the educational decision-making structure at all levels. This situation is now showing signs of change as is evidenced by the growing number of blacks on school boards in the major cities, in school administration, as principals, and as teachers in the ghetto educational systems. These changes accompanied the changing racial composition of big-city schools in the North. Prior to World War II, black involvement in the educational process was largely confined to the South. In many instances this involvement is still at the token level, and in others it reflects on the one hand the general attitude of school administrations that black personnel should be able to handle the problems of black youth, and on the other, the growing refusal of white teachers to accept assignments in schools which have come to be recognized as problem schools. So, by default, black input has been permitted to increase as the situation has gone from bad to worse. But there are those who contend that input in the form of personnel changes alone is not enough to alter the direction in which most ghetto schools appear to be headed.

There is strong evidence which suggests that black parents have traditionally placed greater confidence in the educational process than in any other social process operating in American society in their effort to move up from the bottom rung of the economic ladder. This evidence is no doubt best expressed in the long struggle to eliminate a legal system of segregated education in the South and in the post Brown era (Supreme Court Decision of 1954) to eliminate a system of de facto school segregation in the North and West. After more than 15 years since the passage of that decision, it appears that progress is underway in the South, but the problem of de facto segregation is annually becoming more intense.

The basic principle upon which the school fight was waged was the denial of human dignity, but from a practical point of view it was essentially fought to provide black youth greater access to improved educational opportunities. It was generally thought that with the elimination of racially segregated schools one of the major barriers to economic success would be eliminated. It has been amply demonstrated that the problem is much more complex than that, and even if it were a problem of such simple dimensions, almost no progress has been made in the school systems outside the South toward its solution. Ghetto schools during the previous generation have failed to transform black youth into productive citizens whose lot in life would provide them with the security that has become commonplace for the vast majority of Americans. The educational system cannot be held totally responsible for its failure to respond to the needs of a new generation of black youth, as the educational system simply responds to the will of the body politic.

Racial Isolation in the Public Schools

The strength of racial isolation in the public school system varies regionally, generally as a result of previous legal restraints and the proportion of blacks found in the school system. Even so, it has been demonstrated that a fairly wide range of variations exists among non-Southern cities with similar proportions of blacks attending the public schools. In those cities where blacks constitute 30 to 49 percent of the children enrolled in the public schools, such as Boston, Cincinnati, and Rochester, less than half of those children attend schools which were more than 90 percent black, while in Buffalo and Indianapolis 70 to 80 percent of the black children were enrolled in black schools. Similarly, in cities with blacks constituting fewer than 30 percent of all enrollees, a wide variation prevailed which showed San Francisco with slightly more than 20 percent of its black pupils in racially isolated schools, whereas Milwaukee had more than 70 percent of its pupils in this kind of school environment.[13] The most extreme cases of racial isolation are to be found in those cities where blacks now represent the majority of the school population. St. Louis, Chicago, Baltimore, Cleveland, Philadelphia, and Detroit, in that order, represent the most intense racially isolated school systems outside of the South, and there is a select number of Southern school systems that are less racially isolated than those prevailing in these major ghetto centers.

Efforts at eliminating racial isolation have been all but stymied in most instances, as the neighborhood school has assumed a sanctity during the recent period that did not previously exist. Thus, most of the efforts and schemes which were initiated during the middle sixties have been abandoned or are being only weakly pursued. Southern legislators, sensing the North's resistance to altering the racial balance in its schools, recently attempted to arrange for Northern school systems to be subjected to the same legal requirements of eliminating dual school systems as those imposed upon the

[13] Thomas R. Dye, "Urban School Segregation," *Urban Affairs Quarterly*, Dec., 1968, p. 153.

South. While the ploy was defeated, it was simply an attempt to slow down the process of school desegregation in the South, but at the same time it illustrated the hypocritical position prevailing outside the South.

Racial Change and the Character of the Schools

As schools enter the process of racial transition, they, like the neighborhoods in which they are located, experience a period of conflict and stress. Frequently the transition in the racial composition of the schools occurs more rapidly than does that of the neighborhood. The demographic structure of the school attendance area might influence the rate of change, but in many instances white parents choose to transfer their children to nonneighborhood schools until such time as is convenient for the household to relocate outside of the zone of racial transition. The latter pattern tends to characterize the decisions of parents in both public and nonpublic schools alike. As this process continues in operation, it is inevitable that most big-city school systems outside the South will eventually serve a majority black student population. Once this situation exists, the general quality of education is thought to enter a state of decline. Carey's analysis of the situation in Washington, D.C.'s most intensely segregated zone of black occupancy shows that there exists a negative correlation between experienced teachers and the prevalence of what are described as problem schools. The teachers, it is shown, tend to be male with probationary status.[14] The implication of this condition is a deemphasis on learning and increasing emphasis on maintaining discipline.

Under these conditions teacher-transfer requests are accelerated, resulting in young, inexperienced teachers being concentrated in ghetto schools. Havighurst, in describing the nature of the school environment in the inner-city schools of Chicago, not all of which are black, indicates the job is more difficult, given the nature of the problems which abound in these schools, and that young, experienced teachers fare better in these environments than older, experienced teachers or young, inexperienced teachers.[15] It is rather obvious that a conflict in life styles between students and teachers creates an environment which makes teaching difficult. This leads teachers to write these students off as low educational risks, about which the school can do little. Clark attributes some of the learning-related problems which characterize ghetto schools to the

[14] George W. Carey, Lenore Macomber, and Michael Greenberg, "Educational and Demographic Factors in the Urban Geography of Washington, D.C.," *The Geographical Review*, Oct., 1969, p. 530.

[15] Robert J. Havighurst, *The Public Schools of Chicago,* Board of Education of the City of Chicago, Chicago, 1964, p. 158.

general attitudes of teachers, which grow out of class snobbery, racial snobbery, and ignorance.[16] He states that "children who are treated as if they are uneducable almost invariably become uneducable."[17]

Because of the existing attitudes in American society, ghetto schools eventually acquire staffs that are increasingly black, in the hope of bringing the situation under control and possibly even having some teaching and subsequent learning as a result. But many black teachers, just as their white counterparts, have been socialized in such a way as to absorb the principal dimensions of white middle-class culture and thus, themselves, frequently view students possessing lower-class life styles as unlikely to succeed in the educational system. Thus, while the ghettoization of Northern big-city school systems has provided a growing number of black teachers an opportunity to move into well-paid positions and to gain access to a source of employment which was previously only available in the de jure dual school systems of the South, it has not resulted in the resolution of the internal conflict which prevails in ghetto schools and which is thought to make learning difficult. A St. Louis study recently highlighted this point.

Social Class Conflict and Ghetto Education

Observations were conducted in a St. Louis elementary school located in a school district which was predominantly black, and with a staff that was totally black. The objective of this study was to determine teacher expectation as it affected student performance.[18] The observations were confined to a single classroom and to the same group of students, inclusive of additions and withdrawals, during the kindergarten year and again during the second grade. In both instances the evidence shows that teachers grouped children at a common table in terms of the extent to which they did, or did not, exhibit aspects of middle-class behavior as expressed in physical appearance, interactional behavior, use of language, and a set of social factors that the teacher had acquired from the student's record.[19] The teachers' treatment and subsequent classification of these children was shown to be based on a normative reference group which was middle class—the class category which the teacher herself represented. This led Rist to conclude that: "The organization of the Kindergarten classroom according to the expectation of success or failure after the eighth day of school became the basis for the

16 Kenneth B. Clark, *Dark Ghetto,* Harper & Row, New York, 1965, pp. 127-128.
17 *Ibid.,* p. 128.
18 Ray C. Rist, "Student Social Class and Teacher Expectations: The Self-Fulfilling Prophecy in Ghetto Education," *Harvard Educational Review,* Aug., 1970, pp. 411-451.
19 *Ibid.,* pp. 419-421.

differential treatment of children for the remainder of the school
year."[20] These observations were conducted in a black elementary
school, and it reveals that even in schools which are totally admin-
istered by black personnel that the impact of the dominant culture
results in the relegation of children to the slag heap at a very early
age if they show signs of not conforming to a normative set of values.
Thus, the cultural conflict thesis does seem to possess some measure
of validity beyond that attributed to it by some writers. In school
systems in which this factor might tend to be more pronounced, as in
the case of schools dominated by middle-class white teachers and
lower-class black children, the impact might be even more severe,
even though the behavior elicited may not have the intended effect.

The unwillingness or inability of school systems to overcome the
problems of de facto school segregation, and that unwillingness which
largely revolves around the intolerance of forms of behavior which
differ from the normative forms, has resulted in the introduction of
programs of compensatory education in school systems throughout
the nation. Compensatory programs are largely subsidized under
various Titles of the Elementary and Secondary Education Act of
1965. It was generally agreed that a massive outlay of funds would
be necessary to eliminate some of the learning disabilities and
previous inadequate educational experiences, to teach the black and
other "disadvantaged" Johnny's to read and to adopt a life-style
pattern which would lead to an enhancement of their life chances. It
is said that the Title I program of the Elementary and Secondary
Education Act (ESEA) was an attempt at educational reform that
was not the result of external pressure.[21] As a result of the lack of
external pressure for the program, it was suspect and viewed as an
attempt at a Federal takeover of the public schools. Indeed, the
drafters of the act, somewhat free from external pressure, did specify
on whom the money would be spent. It was designated to be
distributed among school districts characterized by a high incidence
of poverty.[22] While the drafters of the act specified for whom or to
what districts the funds were to be allocated, the programming and
program management aspects of the enterprise were locally controlled
by the state and/or the city. Furthermore, a low-income district was
defined as one having at least 10 poor children. Baron, in a recent
assessment of how ESEA funds were spent in Chicago, concluded
that Title I funds permitted the city of Chicago to increase the per
capita pupil expenditure in the city's black school districts without
the necessity of having to utilize local funds, as a means of closing

[20] *Ibid.*
[21] Jerome T. Murphy, "Politics of Federal Education Reforms," *Harvard Educational Review*, Feb., 1971, p. 27.
[22] *Ibid.,* p. 39.

the gap between per capita pupil expenditures in black and white school districts in the city.[23] While the gap in the per pupil expenditures based on race in the Chicago school system had still not been closed by 1966, it had, through the use of ESEA funds, become smaller. Baron was quick to note that the concentration of young, inexperienced teachers in black schools resulted in reducing the per pupil expenditures in those schools, as teacher salaries account for approximately 80 percent of the cost of operating schools.[24]

Educational operating expenditures in the Chicago public school system tend to vary as function of both race and status. Low-status black schools receive less per school child than do low-status white schools, but low-status white schools receive less per pupil than high-status white schools. Havighurst during the early sixties grouped the public schools of Chicago into four categories. The categories employed largely represented variations in patterns of student behavior and the nature of the education problems found in various parts of the system (Figure 5.5).[25] Most of the schools serving the city's black population were identified as inner-city schools. Inner-city schools were those in which student conduct was considered a serious barrier to teaching. Most white students attended schools which were either high status, mainline, or common man. Each of these was characterized by a different set of life styles having a differential effect upon the promotion and development of an environment conducive to learning. Inner-city schools are those in which most low-income populations are educated. Thus the inner-city schools are the focus of ESEA activity, but there is little evidence to date that Title I programs have had a real impact on altering the quality of education received. Baron has viewed the impact of Title I in the following way:[26]

> Funds can be spent on goods and services as a form of conspicuous consumption or to serve certain ritualistic social purposes other than pedagogic results. The manner in which Title I money has been used falls into this classification. Schools ceremoniously demonstrated that they were doing something—in this case, spending education funds—to meet the needs of discontented black people.

Community Control and a New Role for Ghetto Schools

The continuing inability of ghetto schools to assure a larger propor-

[23] Harold M. Baron, "Race and Status in School Spending: Chicago, 1961-1966," *The Journal of Human Resources,* Winter, 1971, pp. 14-17.

[24] *Ibid.,* p. 9.

[25] Havighurst, *op. cit.,* pp. 145-166.

[26] Baron, *op. cit.,* p. 20.

Figure 5.5 Life-style characteristics and racial identity of Chicago's public schools. (Sources: Adapted from Robert J. Havighurst, *The Public Schools of Chicago*, Chicago Board of Education, 1964; and Brian J. L. Berry and Katherine B. Smith, *Down From the Summit*, Center for Urban Studies, University of Chicago, 1969)

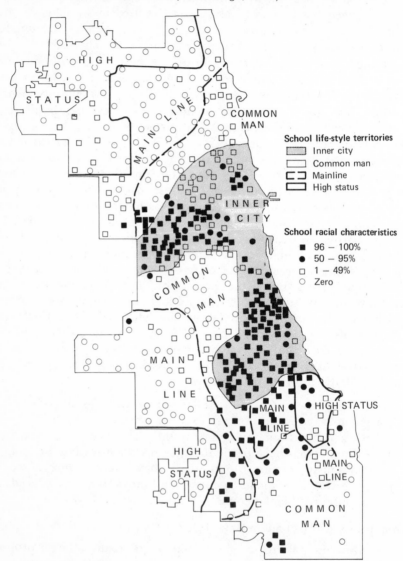

tion of black youths attending them that they can look forward to leading a productive life has resulted in a number of interventionist strategies being posed by local community groups. A growing number of groups feel that parents should play a more important role in the decision-making which will affect their children's lives.

Hamilton thinks the ghetto school should play a central role in ghetto community development, with schools performing a more diverse set of functions and involving a wider variety of people than they do currently. He likewise believes that educational achievement will have to be measured in terms other than verbal achievement and mathematical skills, but to them must be added the success of the school in promoting a positive self-image.[27] In order to accomplish this latter goal, it is thought that a more sensitive set of teachers should be sought who understand ghetto culture and who are less prone to shatter a child's self-image by emphasizing the lack of legitimacy of the traditions and values of his parents and peers.

Many think that major school reform will be necessary to overcome many of the obstacles which currently aid in assuring that the ghetto school will be unable to accomplish the objectives of the American educational system. Increasingly, calls for community control over local school systems are being heard. This represents the latest strategy of ghetto residents in the game of the politics of education to make the schools more responsive to their demands. Efforts at community control at this point have been only experimental. The best-known attempt of community control was the short-lived experience of the Ocean Hill-Brownsville district in Brooklyn's black ghetto. Mr. Rhody McCoy, the administrator for that unit, revealed that there was a sharp decrease in the extent of vandalism, pupil absence, teacher absence, and teacher turnover during the year in which the experiment was conducted.[28] The attempt, like others which will follow, tended to generate conflict between teachers' unions and local community groups, resulting in the formation of new coalitions designed to support one interest group or another. A principal representative of the New York teacher bargaining organization is of the opinion that district size has little or nothing to do with pupil achievement and the matter is essentially related to class, thus minimizing the advantages that are thought to accrue as a result of local control.

The local control fight is not likely to be won by ghetto residents, as it represents a major departure in the way things are done in big city school systems. While the fight may not be won, some concessions are likely to be granted. Detroit recently re-districted the schools in such a way as to indicate that it was aware of the changing attitudes toward the manner in which its schools were being operated. It is too soon to say that the newly devised plan for electing school board members, based on membership in a local

---

27 Charles V. Hamilton, "Race and Education: A Search for Legitimacy," *Harvard Educational Review*, Fall, 1968, p. 673.

28 Mario D. Fantini, "Participation, Decentralization, Community Control and Quality Education," *Teachers College Record*, Sept., 1969, pp. 106-107.

district in Detroit, represents a trend, but it is nevertheless evident that there are those who feel that a more effective educational delivery system can be structured in the ghetto through increased involvement of community residents.

GHETTO HEALTH-CARE SYSTEMS

The availability of health care in the nation's ghettos has only recently begun to be formally recognized as a problem of enormous magnitude. This new turnabout in interest is partially associated with the increased pressure that black and other low-income populations have imposed upon the health delivery system. This new pressure is a result of Federal intervention (1965) and is associated with the passage of the Medicare and Medical Assistance Act (Medicaid).

The Use of Health-Care Facilities by Ghetto Residents

Prior to the passage of this specified health-care legislation, the general concensus was that low-income people and black people in particular led such crisis-ridden lives that attention to their health received low priority—a problem that somehow had to be overcome. It is true that many low-income black people, especially those who had reached maturity in the rural South, have assumed that poor health was simply another aspect of their lot in life over which they had no control. But new evidence shows that many of the explanations which attributed low-income black populations' underutilization of medical services to dimensions of group culture are fallacious.[29] There is little question that the role of culture does account for some of the limited use of health facilities by blacks, but more often than not, the cultural factor represents an interactional response rather than a simple lack of faith in medical services or the low priority given to health care.

The combined increase in the number of both medically indigent and nonmedically indigent black populations in the nation's central cities, occurring at a time when the general population is economically able to purchase an increasing volume of medical care, has overtaxed our outdated health delivery system. The present system has grown up with the nation and has essentially taken care of the ills of the more affluent segment of the population through fee for service medicine. Numerous innovations are currently being considered as means of providing assurance that the health needs of all of the people can be met. It is obvious at this point that the existing medical delivery system will not be able to service the nation's

---

[29] John M. Goering and Rodney M. Coe, "Cultural Versus Situational Explanations of the Medical Behavior of the Poor," *Social Science Quarterly*, Sept., 1970, pp. 313-317.

population effectively through the existing single-class system of fee for service. Fee for service must be augmented by other alternatives and promising measures if good medical care for all segments of the nation's population is to be realized. Some of the recommendations for improved services which have begun to come forward would give ghetto residents a voice in determining the structure and operation of the system. If citizen participation is indeed effective in the structuring of health delivery systems, ghetto and other low-income populations should be provided with the kind of access to medical care which has not been generally available to this population.

The Health Status of the Black Population

It is universally agreed that low-income populations are among the most unhealthy groups in the nation. Inattention and/or lack of access to health services confound the plight of the poor by making it impossible to escape from this category. The notion that the ghetto represents a developing area within the most economically advanced nation in the world takes on added credence when the health status of the black population is measured against that of the white population. In 1960 it was shown that blacks lagged 40 years behind whites in level of health attainment,[30] and the gap was shown to have increased during each 20-year period since 1900. Fein concluded from his investigation that blacks and whites move over the same range of experience—in this instance, health—at different rates. Until real progress is made in accelerating the speed with which blacks move through these experiences, the gap will continue to expand in the future.

The infant mortality rate is generally thought to represent the most sensitive health indicator of level of economic development. In 1962 the nonwhite infant mortality rate was 90 percent greater than the white infant level.[31] There is evidence that the absolute level of infant mortality in big-city ghettos is on the decline, but it is still much higher than one would expect in a nation where medical services are among the best in the world.

The knowledge of the differential impact of the major killers among blacks and whites is fairly commonplace. Among black males, diseases of early infancy, influenza and pneumonia, and hypertensive heart disease are listed among the five major killers, while only influenza and pneumonia are among the five ranking killers of white males and even here the rate is almost one-half that characterizing

[30] Rashi Fein, "An Economic and Social Profile of the Negro American," *Daedalus,* Fall, 1965, pp. 816-818.
[31] *Ibid.,* p. 816.

the nonwhite level.[32]   Homicide, the tenth ranking cause of death among black males is not one of the major killers of white males. The high incidence of homicide is thought to reflect psychosocial implications of the black man's historical position in American society, while the three previously mentioned ranking killers reflect both economic and psychological pressures. Any realistic efforts at health planning within the ghetto context would address itself to the needs of that population, based upon the observed incidence of those diseases and actions which result in reducing black life expectancy.

The Status of Medical Services Within the Ghetto

Ghetto areas are increasingly becoming medical wastelands as the number of primary-care physicians in these areas continues to diminish. Primary-care physicians include general practitioners, internists, and pediatricians. As zones in cities become increasingly black, there is a corresponding decrease in the number of physicians available to serve them. This lack of availability of physicians at the local level is the result of a shrinkage in the number of primary-care physicians, as more and more medical practitioners are becoming medical specialists, and the lack of black physicians to replace the white physicians who practiced in the area prior to its undergoing racial change. In Chicago black physicians account for only 3.5 percent of all physicians, with the result that more than half of all black patients are being cared for by white physicians.[33] The decline in the number of physicians in the ghetto has resulted in black patients having to travel a greater distance to secure a physicians's service. It is the distance factor which seriously affects the extent to which black residents utilize physicians' services.

In a recent analysis of the availability of primary-care physicians in the city of Baltimore, it was shown that the city had a mean rate of primary-care providers of 160 per 100,000, but there were 15 census tracts of neighborhood size in the city which had no primary-care physicians.[34] These tracts were all concentrated in low-income inner-city areas. Among the districts established for this analysis (there were 15 covering the metropolitan area), one low-income district's rate for primary care was 25.8 per 100,000, a far cry from the 504.1 rate which characterized the district with the

[32] St. Clair Drake, "The Social and Economic Status of the Negro in the United States," *Daedalus,* Fall, 1965, p. 790.

[33] Richard L. Morrill, Robert J. Erickson, and Philip Rees, "Factors Influencing Distances Traveled to Hospitals," *Economic Geography,* April, 1970, p. 166.

[34] Alma W. McMillan, et al., "Assessing the Balance of Physician Manpower in a Metropolitan Area," *Public Health Reports,* Nov., 1970, p. 1007.

largest number of practitioners, the downtown office district (Figure 5.6).

In 1961 the level of primary-care providers in Boston was already considerably below the level of care available in Baltimore in 1968. The physical proximity of primary-care physicians to low-income black populations is not so much the problem in this instance as that

Figure 5.6 Distribution of primary-care physicians and proximity to the Balti-more ghetto, 1968. (Source: W. McMillan, et al., "Assessing the Balance of Physician Manpower in a Metropolitan Area," *Public Health Reports*, Nov. 1970)

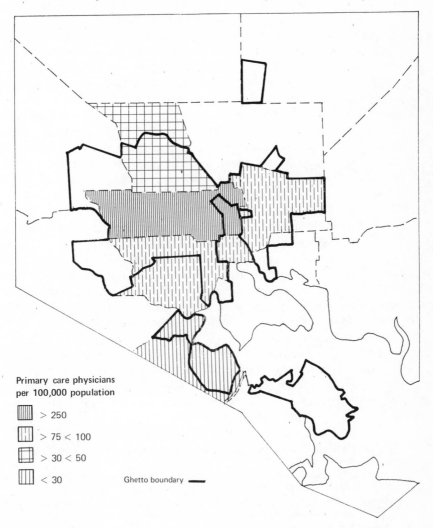

Primary care physicians
per 100,000 population

▨ > 250

▨ > 75 < 100

▨ > 30 < 50

▨ < 30   Ghetto boundary ▬

physicians tend to be clustered in "physicians' areas" which are often found in old office districts near low-income areas.[35] But physical access in this instance does not guarantee personal access. Bashur and others commenting on a similar locational configuration in Cleveland stated, "The high peaks of hospitals and of physicians are almost literally across the street from the major Black enclave, yet we know the utilization of blacks to be low."[36] The difference in ghetto scale in Chicago and Boston promotes differential access to physicians' areas.

Hospital services like physician's services are both inadequate in quality and volume within the ghetto context. Unlike physicians, hospitals exist within ghetto space, but they are seldom responsive to the needs of local populations. Hospitals representing a highly capitalized investment do not have the same kind of mobility as do physicians who can alter their locations as a means of adjusting to the changing spatial patterns of their clientele. Hospitals on the other hand, with their fixed location, depend on the clients to make the adjustment by traveling greater distances to secure hospital care. Most of the larger hospital facilities tend to be centrally located within the nation's urban complexes, thereby placing them within easy travel range of the black and the poor, who tend to represent the dominant population in the surrounding environment. But because of cost, prejudice, and the absence of black physicians on the staffs at these hospitals, black access is frequently denied. While major hospitals are often located in close proximity to the black ghetto, they seldom serve that population effectively.

Private hospital care has often been designed to provide service for a specific clientele, although other populations have not been excluded from access to these services. Ethnic and religious groups have been active in the health-care field, and many hospitals in metropolitan areas are supported by religious groups. Among Chicago's 119 hospitals, 42 percent have religious affiliations and 4.2 percent or five institutions were designed to serve a black clientele.[37] The latter situation reflects a social history of exclusion resulting in the necessity to develop parallel institutions, aside from an overt desire to develop such facilities, which were generally underfunded and thereby providing inadequate care.

In the Chicago case and in most large metropolitan complexes, ghetto patients are overly dependent upon overcrowded public

[35] Leon S. Robertson, "On the Intraurban Ecology of Primary Care Physicians," *Social Science and Medicine,* Vol. 4, 1970, pp. 231-235.

[36] Rashid L. Bashur, et al., "The Application of the Three-Dimensional Analogue Models to the Distribution of Medical Care Facilities," *Medical Care,* Sept.-Oct., 1970, p. 406.

[37] Robert Earickson, *The Spatial Behavior of Hospital Patients,* Department of Geography, University of Chicago, 1970, pp. 52-53.

health-care facilities. De Vise indicates that one-half million of Chicago's more than one million blacks are effectively shut off from all but one of that city's hospitals.[38] Many hospitals within or having easy access to the ghetto have closed their outpatient clinics and serve blacks as emergency patients only.[39] Emergency departments are generally the least well staffed and financed departments within hospitals, therefore, providing black patients, who have only limited access, inferior service. This situation has led many black patients to make use of the public charity hospital to which they may admit themselves. Morrill has described the situation in Chicago in the following way:[40] "The only hospital which normally allows such admissions is Cook County Hospital, an enormous, congested, and unfriendly institution, removed from large portions of the black ghetto by a long and arduous journey."

Many of the older and smaller hospitals located with easy access to the ghetto population are beginning to show signs of willingness to have black physicians serve as members of their staffs. In some instances, this is no doubt an outgrowth of growing vacancy rates, as white physicians increasingly become affiliated with small modern hospitals of the community type which are rising in suburbia. Thus, by default, in some instances, black physicians are acquiring staff privileges at hospitals which are indeed attempting to adjust to the situation in which they find themselves, a decreasing white clientele and white physicians' exercise of their greater number of options as to choice of hospital staff assignment. Figure 5.7 illustrates the geography of black physician hospital staff appointments in the city of Milwaukee.

The Rise of Neighborhood Health-Care Centers

During the last five years, changes have been occurring within the health professions which could lead to an improvement in the availability of health care for ghetto residents. Emphasis has begun to be shifted away from the hospital as the preeminent unit in the health delivery system. The hospital orientation as the source of both medical training and medical care has dominated American medicine for more than two generations. The inability of the hospital to handle a growing diversity of health-care needs, ranging from a changing social environment to the development of new health insurance programs, has led to an emphasis on the expansion of neighborhood health-care centers. These centers, it is assumed, will provide more effective treatment for the ambulatory patient who

38 Pierre de Vise, "The Social Pressures," *Hospitals, J.A.H.A.,* Feb. 1, 1971, p. 51.
39 *Ibid.,* p. 51.
40 Morrill, *op cit.,* p. 168.

does not require hospitalization and within a social environment which is nonthreatening.

Figure 5.7   Black physicians with staff privileges at Milwaukee area hospitals.

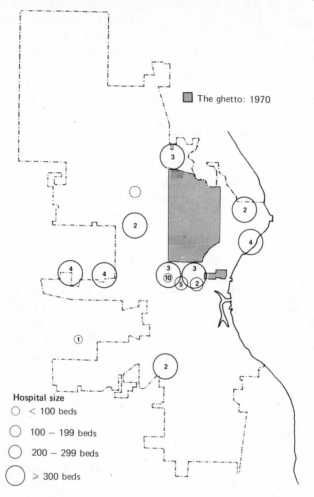

Number of black physicians shown by number in circle

The shift in emphasis which has resulted in the rise of a number of neighborhood health centers, in both rural and urban settings, is associated with an increasing concern for the delivery of health services.[41] Most of the centers have emerged since 1965 and are supported by funding from the Office of Economic Opportunity (OEO). The centers tend to be concentrated in the major urban

[41] H. Jack Geiger and Roger D. Cohen, "Trends in Health Care Delivery Systems," *Inquiry*, March, 1971, pp. 32-35.

centers of the East, but centers are to be found in at least one urban complex in each major geographic region. After five years of program development, 49 OEO-sponsored centers have evolved, the first represented by the Columbia Point Project in Boston.[42] In California, both Watts and East Palo Alto have been recipients of a neighborhood health center attuned to the needs of a black population that previously had only limited access to health care facilities.

One of the more significant outgrowths of the rise of the neighborhood health-care centers is that there is local involvement in the structure and design of the center and its operation. Medical professionals, who still tend to play the dominant role in the neighborhood health-care structure, are reluctantly beginning to allow neighborhood representatives a greater voice in the decision-making structure. A modicum of community control is much better developed here than is the case with the educational system.

Another advantage of community involvement in the neighborhood health center structure is that it promotes broad-scale community welfare which transcends health care. In the planning of most neighborhood health centers, attempts are made to seek meaningful employment opportunities for local residents in the operation of the center. Here, efforts are made to provide opportunities in the paraprofessional area as a means of providing a job opportunity ladder. While blacks have found employment in central-city hospitals throughout the nation, they are generally concentrated in the housekeeping department with little opportunity for advancement. Efforts of this sort have not generally been available in the established health-care structure.

Recently an attempt was made to tie the development of a medical complex to the necessity of involving local blacks in the building of the medical center and subsequently training local residents for paraprofessional positions within the institution. This effort was met with heavy objections from medical professionals who had not anticipated the necessity of bargaining at this level to acquire a site for the construction of a medical school complex. The above situation refers to the Newark Medical School controversy, a situation which is said to have been one of the factors which led to the Newark riot of 1967. The negotiations for the medical school site were initiated in 1966, but it was not until 1968 that the negotiators were willing to accept the notion of local citizen involvement, at least in terms of employment and training which is usually built into the neighborhood health center structure.[43]

[42] Jerome L. Schwartz, "Early Histories of Selected Neighborhood Health Centers," *Inquiry*, Dec., 1970, pp. 3-5.

[43] Leonard J. Duhl and Nancy J. Steele, "Newark: Community or Chaos," *Journal of Applied Behavioral Science*, Vol. 5, No. 4, 1969, pp. 537-572.

Neighborhood health centers could reduce the pressure on hospitals at a time when hospital costs are at a peak, and at the same time make primary care available within a local area. It is generally recognized that, while many advantages are to be gained from these efforts, such centers do not represent a panacea. Nevertheless, the embryonic rise of these centers does permit both an improvement in access to health care and a voice in the determination of the nature and quality of that care, as well as selected participation in the delivery of care.

PUBLIC SAFETY

There have long been attempts, with some minimal success, on the part of black people to make the educational system more responsive to their needs. Attempts at altering the structure of health care are more recent, but there is evidence, too, that the health-care system is beginning to respond to a changing set of circumstances in a way that will prove advantageous to the black and the poor. Of the three major delivery systems chosen for observation, the only one which appears nonresponsive to the needs of ghetto residents is the system of public safety and/or protection. In this instance, public safety is restricted to those services that are delivered to the ghetto by members of the police department. It is common knowledge that the nature of police-ghetto relations has made an effective delivery system all but impossible.

THE GHETTO ENVIRONMENT AND SAFETY

Most writers who touch upon this topic do so from a point of departure which tends to emphasize the unusually high crime rates which prevail within the ghetto context. While this is a valid point of departure, it seldom encompasses the desire of the ghetto resident to reside within an atmosphere of safety free from the fear of personal danger which is accorded other segments of society. The crime orientation generally reflects the fear of the larger population which happens to live in close proximity to the ghetto, whose business makes it periodically necessary for them to visit the ghetto, or who have capital investments there, rather than the concerns of permanent residents who are both the perpetrators and the victims of crime.

The Ghetto Resident and the Problem of Safety

From the perspective of the ghetto resident the problem is much more than one of simply bringing crime under control by any means necessary; it is one of providing an effective system of public safety which not only guarantees the physical safety of persons and property, but psychic safety as well. The providers of public safety, it is argued, score low on the first point, frequently because of the lack of cooperation of ghetto residents, and poorer still on the second because of the status accorded the average ghetto resident by the providers of the service—the police. Needless to say, the ghetto is the most intensely occupied segment of urban America, and the least well protected, at least in terms of effective protection. If the ghetto is to lose its identity as the jungle in which criminal behavior permeates every nook and cranny, it will require a more effective safety delivery system—one which will reflect the concerns and fears of its resident population rather than simply the concerns and fears of an extraterritorial population.

Low-income zones within cities are almost universally zones within which nonlegal activities tend to abound. Many attribute the flourishing of such activities to the qualities of both the physical and social environment within the area of residence. The squalid tenements, with their high density populations and correspondingly limited amounts of per person space; the low incomes of the resident population, which stifle access to those commodities and services which are deemed essential in urban America; and the patterns of behavior, frequently considered pathological, which evolve out of such circumstances: all these characteristics lead to incursions into the arena of illegal and extralegal activities. When such zones are also occupied by residents who have been left out of the system on grounds other than those which apply to the population at large, the situation is made even more difficult. Thus the physical environment of the ghetto, coupled with forms of behavior which reflect group norms and antipathies, leads to frequent confrontations with the law.

In this instance, the problem has become so complex that it becomes almost impossible to separate the effect of internal and external physical environment from the effect of internal and external social environment on the behavior which leads to the victimization of others and encounters with the law. Likewise, the spillover effects associated with other institutions operating within this context tend to aggravate the problem.

The ghetto is more heterogeneous than most other social zones within the city. The mechanism which promotes ghettoization leads to a more heterogeneous population mix, aside from the fact of racial identity, than that which occurs elsewhere. While zones of economic variation are found within the ghetto, they only tend to reveal themselves as the ghetto expands over space. Thus, within this spatial realm, a somewhat heterogeneous population emerges in terms of economic identity, a situation which frequently leads to internal group conflict.

It is this internal group conflict that points up the fact that the social system has promoted and abetted a situation which leads to a predator/prey condition from which there is no escape. High rates of unemployment lead those who are unemployed to rob the employed; those who have, to be burglarized by the have-nots. The need to shore up one's faltering identity structure leads to assault, and the instability associated with ghetto family life frequently leads to homicide or lesser physical abuse. Acts of this sort are commonplace, but those most often victimized are one's neighbors who also happen to be black. Of those crimes that are recognized as index crimes and the ones upon which the nation's crime rates are based, robbery is the only one in which the perpetrator is most often black and the victim most often white. Thus, the black contribution to the nation's rising crime rate is essentially represented by an increase in the number of homicides, aggravated assaults, rapes, burglary, larcenies, and auto thefts, in which the victims are of the same race as those engaging in the act.

One can hardly believe that it was an increase in the level of criminal activity within the ghetto, in which blacks have been victimized by other blacks, that has led to the politicians' cry for "law and order" or the need to eliminate "crime in the streets." The social system operates in such a way as to make blacks reluctant to join the crusade against crime in the street, because one is aware that the euphemism is a racially loaded one, which, in a symbolic sense, would pit black against blacks at a time when there is a call for greater unity. Thus, the nature of racial conflict in the nation in general makes it psychologically difficult to raise the same cries as less victimized segments of the white population when it is realized that the providers of protection tend not to identify with those who require the greatest protection.

It is the nature of the social system and the way it impinges upon the ghetto resident, both in terms of internal and external effect, that no doubt led Clark to describe the ghetto as pathological and to comment as follows:[44]

> Neither instability nor crime can be controlled by police vigilance or by reliance on the alleged deterring forces of legal punishment, for individual crimes are to be understood more as symptoms of the contagious sickness of the community itself than as a result of inherent criminal or deliberate viciousness.

The pathological argument has been picked up more recently by a number of writers who tend to ignore the social context within which the ghetto exists and who subsequently attribute the behavior

[44] Clark, *op. cit.*, p. 81.

found therein to human frailty—an argument which is unacceptable to many writers who view the situation holistically.

The overriding issue here is whether the ghetto can be made safe, given the variety of forces which act upon it to make it a natural breeding ground for crime. Can the present system of safety perform effectively within the existing social context? While there is no absolute answer to this question, it appears that there are inherent weaknesses in the way the present system addresses itself to the needs of the black community.

THE SAFETY DELIVERY SYSTEM

Unlike the two systems previously discussed, this one is seemingly insensitive to the demands of local populations. This insensitivity derives from the fact that the police department is a self-regulating agency or at least a quasi self-regulating agency. In neither of the other systems does one find the kind of employee-organizational loyalty that is found within the police force. The strong bond of loyalty works against efforts designed to promote adjustments in the operation of the force to ameliorate grievances which have grown up between the community and the force. These factors, added to the value placed on conformity which seems to derive from the personality needs of individual policemen and the dictates of police culture as well, inevitably lead to conflict between the police and ghetto residents.

Police-Community Relations

Ghetto residents frequently perceive the police as members of an occupying force, who are present in the ghetto to protect the interests of a nonresidential white population whose value system they conform to and uphold. The police, who are most often selected from working-class segments of the population, view the present structure of American society as highly desirable.[45] Persons possessing attributes which deny that they have absorbed the principal dimensions of middle-class American culture provoke suspicion and are subject to careful police scrutiny. Blacks possessing lower-class life styles, which are expressed overtly in a variety of ways, are logical objects of suspicion, given the way the police culture operates.

The recent upsurge on the part of black youth in their defiance of the symbolic authority accorded the police has tended to aggravate police-community relations. Evidence of the erosion of the authority image is associated with the increased frequency of public

[45] Daniel H. Swett, "Cultural Bias in the American Legal System," *Law and Society Review*, Aug., 1969, pp. 87-88.

use of disparaging epithets in psychically attacking members of the force. The police have recoiled at this growing lack of respect and have assumed a defensive posture, a factor which no doubt had led to a stepped-up psychic attack on the part of blacks and other youths who frequently come into contact with the police in a conflict situation. Symonds, in describing the police personality which is strongly oriented toward conformity and homage to authority, indicates that signs of being disliked can place one under increased emotional stress.[46] A recent survey of the attitudes of police in 13 cities showed that they perceived 31 percent of the black population to hold hostile attitudes toward them with another 36 percent being viewed as indifferent.[47] It was found that young officers exceeded older members of the force in the perception of black hostility. Needless to say, the growing arrogance of black youth has aggravated the strained relations between the deliverers of service and the recipients of it.

Police, while generally denying accusations of racial bias, often behave in such a way vis-a-vis blacks that the group's perception of the police is that of a controlling force motivated by racist tendencies rather than a body which is present in the community to render services. Skolnick is of the opinion that the police think of themselves as being honest in their dealings with members of the black community by generally being above board in revealing the general views held by society toward black people.[48] Thus, in the view of the police, the use of ethnic humor and racial epithets do not reflect bias, but simply the status which society accords the group.

It has been necessary in some instances for chiefs to hand down directives to beat patrolmen to discontinue use of epithets which might be interpreted as racially offensive. A documented history of psychic attacks on low-status populations is now being met by counterattacks in kind, a situation which fails to ameliorate the long-standing conflict. Though the situation continues to worsen, many police forces refuse to accept the necessity for developing effective community relations programs. Mendelsohn reports that "there is no support whatever among white officers for improved community relations; indeed, far and away the most popular response calls for a better trained, better equipped, and larger force and stricter law enforcement."[49]

[46] Martin Symonds, "Emotional Hazards of Police Work," *The American Journal of Psychoanalysis,* Vol. 30, 1970, pp. 155-158.

[47] W. Eugene Groves and Peter H. Rossi, "Police Perceptions of a Hostile Ghetto," *American Behavioral Sciences,* Vol. 13, Nos. 5 and 6, 1970, p. 732.

[48] Jerome Skolnick, *Justice Without Trial,* John Wiley & Sons, Inc., New York, 1966, pp. 80-83.

[49] Robert A. Mendelsohn, "Police-Community Relations," *American Behavioral Science,* Vol. 30, Nos. 5 and 6, 1970, p. 747.

In those communities where such programs do exist, they are often considered inadequate. Even in San Francisco where an enlightened community-relations effort was initiated involving representatives of the force and grass-roots community persons, the effort eventually failed.[50] It was revealed that blacks soon recognized that the impact of the community-relations effort did not extend beyond those policemen who were directly involved in the program, a fact which indicated that a half-hearted effort, however sincere, was not enough to convince the black community that the police were really willing to turn over a new leaf.

The Dilemma of the Black Policeman

Black policemen, it has been found, while having adopted the police culture, perceive the black community to be less hostile toward the police than do their white counterparts. Some writers contend that black policemen tend to conform even more rigidly to the code of police ethics than white policemen, because of their desire to be fully accepted by their professional peers. But there is growing evidence that black officers are more and more beginning to empathize with the community as a result of the realization that their job is made more difficult because of the general view held in the black community toward the police.

Black professional police associations are beginning to emerge as counterparts of other ethnic police associations. Increasingly, these groups are adopting a militant stance, an assumed response to what they recognize as improper or at least intemperate conduct of white officers in their dealings with ghetto residents. These associations are often viewed negatively by the police administration, and individual black officers are jeopardizing their careers on the force by having the temerity to challenge the prescribed behavior of the police which has grown out of the police culture.

It is conditions such as this which place the black policeman in a real dilemma, subject to increasing stress and eventual job abandonment or loss. Similarly, the poor image of the police in the ghetto has worked against young black males seeking career opportunities as members of the force. Efforts are currently underway in a number of cities to increase the number of black patrolmen on the force. But unless the image of the police held by residents is altered, the job of attracting blacks into this occupational niche is likely to be difficult indeed. The number and percentage of black policemen vary widely from city to city, with those cities having a large proportion of blacks in their total population showing up best (Table 5.1). The police culture and ghetto culture appear to be at odds, and unless the

50 Robert J. Condlin, "Citizens, Police, and Polarization: Are Perceptions More Important than Facts?", *Journal of Urban Law*, Vol. 47, Issue 3, 1969-70, pp. 667-672.

situation is ameliorated, the black community can expect little in the way of improvements in the delivery of service.

Table 5.1 Black police in key cities

Cities	% black	Total police force	Total black police	% black police
Washington, D.C.	71.1	4,944	1,797	35.9
Newark	54.2	1,500	225	15.0
Gary	52.8	415	130	31.0
Atlanta	51.3	942	260	28.0
Baltimore	46.4	3,300	420	13.0
New Orleans	45.0	1,359	83	6.1
Detroit	43.7	5,100	567	12.0
Wilmington, Del.	43.6	277	32	11.5
Birmingham, Ala.	42.0	660	13	1.9
St. Louis, Mo.	40.9	2,221	326	14.0
Portsmouth, Va.	39.9	195	14	7.5
Jackson, Miss.	39.3	270	17	6.2
Memphis	38.9	1,090	55	5.0
Cleveland	38.3	2,445	191	7.7
Mobile, Ala.	35.5	277	36	13.3
Oakland, Cal.	34.5	713	34	4.7
Winston-Salem, N.C.	34.3	300	20	6.6
Shreveport, La.	33.9	345	25	7.2
Philadelphia, Pa.	33.6	7,242	1,347	18.6
Chicago	32.6	12,678	2,100	16.5
Dayton, Ohio	30.5	422	22	4.1
Hartford, Conn.	27.9	500	60	12.0
Pittsburgh, Pa.	20.2	1,640	105	6.4
Dallas, Tex.	24.9	1,640	32	1.9
Miami, Fla.	22.7	719	74	10.0
New York City	21.2	31,700	2,400	7.5
Los Angeles	17.9	6,705	350	5.2
Boston	16.3	2,807	60	2.1
Milwaukee	14.7	2,098	50	2.3
San Francisco	13.4	1,800	90	5.0

Source: Ebony, May, 1971, p. 124.

The Question of Community Control

The conflict between the police and the ghetto which continues unabated has once again led to demands for community control. Nowhere is community control likely to be more strongly resisted, and there is little evidence that control of the police by the black community is likely to become a reality. At this point there seems to have been no serious effort to evaluate the potential of community control to improve the delivery of service to the ghetto. Thus it is unclear just what the impact of community control might have on the minimization of crime and the provision of a safe environment. The question and the problems are not going to simply fade away, so measures which today are considered radical might surely be experimented with tomorrow if the situation continues to grow worse.

CONCLUSIONS

The rapid growth of black populations in the nation's major central cities, and the subsequent ghettoization, has led to greater demands for political involvement, including black representation in the full range of governmental decision structures. As central cities proceed to be transformed into communities possessing a black majority, or near majority, and a decreasing white minority, the possibility of having a black citizen serve as mayor is enhanced. Black mayors can be expected to become more commonplace in the near future, but the task of ameliorating the fiscal crisis in which these cities find themselves is likely to become even more difficult. Black control of city hall and a lack of white understanding and indifference in the statehouse could make the job of mayor a frustrating one.

The increase in the absolute size of central-city black populations looks as if it might lessen rather than strengthen black political representation at the national level. The actual absolute loss of central-city populations will make it necessary to alter the geographic configuration of congressional districts in such a way as to dilute black political strength in those zones where the potential for strength was derived through the process of spatial clustering. In the final analysis, though, gains are likely to be made in those communities which are just now arriving at a critical threshold in terms of the population size necessary to support a congressional representative. Thus we might see a loss in congressional representation in those cities possessing superghettos, while temporary gains might accrue to those cities whose black population has just transcended the critical population threshold, provided that a politically optimal spatial residential pattern has emerged.

The geography of the black population within major metropolitan systems will ultimately determine the possibility of blacks succeeding to formal political office on anything other than a token basis. With this fact in mind, the individual black householder will have to weigh his decision to locate among several alternate choices within the metropolis in terms of the perceived political advantages associated with ghettoization, as against alternative advantages perceived to be associated with nonghetto residence, if this latter option presents itself.

To date, most black political officeholders have emerged from the ranks of the black middle class; a parallel situation exists for the white officeholder. The principal difference is that most whites in urban America are middle class, at least in terms of economic status, whereas most blacks are not. This has led some to say that the black office holder does not effectively represent his clientele because of goal conflicts which are imbedded in class differences. It is quite possible that this latter accusation is false, but nevertheless it is evident that a new style of political leader is emerging in the ghetto who is attempting to speak to the needs of the black masses. Some of these political leaders are working outside the formal political structure and possibly should not be identified as political leaders, but certainly must be recognized as forces to which the political system must respond.

A review of the operation of three ghetto delivery systems was undertaken in an attempt to determine if ghetto political power had been effectively utilized in making these systems responsive to the needs of its resident population. It was generally found that the ghetto had not been able to influence the manner in which these systems operated through the formal political structure. In part, this was true because of the lack of congruence between ghetto scale and the service system scale, a factor which permitted these systems to remain only moderately sensitive to the needs of the black population. Formal attempts to alter the way these systems operate in ghetto space have been successful only when the impetus for change was initiated outside the ghetto. A case in point are the changes which are beginning to emerge in the health delivery system, most of which represent the influence of external variables. It is true that ghetto residents do not yet have the power to address themselves to altering the operation of systems which are basic to their survival. As a matter of fact, they may never have this power, given the complex interaction of social, economic, and political variables. Nevertheless, efforts which show signs of making delivery systems more effective in servicing ghetto populations should not be discontinued. Unless the ghetto is able to muster enough power to influence key decision-makers and until it is recognized that the ghetto population is not monolithic, the delivery systems which operate within the nation's central cities will continue to poorly serve that segment of the population which threatens to become the dominant one, so long as the process of ghettoization continues. With continued ghettoization, the cries for community control are likely to increase in volume as the frustration associated with ghetto living becomes ever more pervasive. If ghettoization does not promote some measure of self control, then the colonial analogue which has been employed by some to describe the ghetto begins to take on added meaning.

CHAPTER 6

THE GHETTO
AND BEYOND

The living space which urban black Americans have acquired over the last several generations has been identified with increasing frequency as a ghetto. There is no major metropolitan system in the nation without its ghetto, although the scale will vary as a function of the housing demand of the black population in a given place. Thus, depending upon the size of the black population, the ghetto as a territorial entity may extend over only a few contiguous blocks, as in the case of Salt Lake City, or over many square miles, as in the case of Chicago. Scale, then, is simply a problem of stage of ghetto development, the rate of growth of the black population, and the physical layout of the city itself. While, conceptually, variations in ghetto scale are of only limited interest, it is the problematic aspects of scale that cause public officials and institutional caretakers to be aware of the ghetto's existence.

THE RIGIDITY OF THE SOCIO-SPATIAL SYSTEM

There is little evidence that the ghetto as a territorial entity is likely to disappear from American cities during the next generation. But as the scale of the ghetto changes, the public officials in central cities and those in outlying suburban communities intensify their debates over who should shoulder the fiscal responsibility for providing social services for ghetto populations. None of the social support arguments have been as heated as those which revolve around the locational aspect of black population distribution within the metropolitan system. Now that suburban populations hold the balance of political power in the nation, it appears that the Federal government is becoming increasingly supportive of the suburban perspective. That perspective tends to view the central city as the natural domain of the black population. It now appears that blacks will possibly be confined to central-city locations, under conditions of economic discrimination rather than overt racial discrimination, if recent court actions are a good indication of things to come. The question of "where we shall live," then, is just as valid today as it was when it was posed by the Commission on Race and Housing in 1958.

The Present Intensity of Spatial Segregation

It is possible that after the social ecologists have had the opportunity to analyze 1970 census block statistics, it will be shown that the pattern of residential segregation based on race is only slightly less intense than it was in 1960. This should come as no surprise. But the reduction of that intensity is likely to be so minor as hardly to have altered the flow of outcomes associated with the ghettoization process. Almost every ghetto in America added to its territorial realm during the previous 10 years. Downs has indicated that field surveys undertaken in Chicago show that approximately three blocks move weekly from predominantly white to predominantly black occupancy.[1] Since the process appears to continue unabated, what are the hard decisions that must be made?

Residential Options and Racial-Class Conflict

Already decisions are being made in the public and private sectors as a means of maintaining some kind of desirable equilibrium condition designed to maintain the status quo, or as Downs has said, to perpetuate the "law of cultural dominance."[2] It seems somewhat paradoxical that the Supreme Court would rule that no citizen of the United States might be barred from moving from one state to another and yet a generation later rule that access to place could indirectly be determined by one's economic status. The latter situation is reminiscent of practices previously described in distinguishing the South from the non-South ia allocating living space to blacks.

In this instance a community can determine its social-class character by previously specifying the lower value limit of housing to be developed within the bounds of the territory under its control. In this way the burden is shifted from access to housing to access to territory. Thus, the freedom of gross movement defined as interstate

[1] Anthony Downs, "Alternative Futures for the American Ghetto," *Daedalus,* Fall, 1968, p. 1333.

[2] *Ibid.,* pp. 1338-1341.

migration that was provided by the courts is being threatened by restrictions on interurban movement by the same legal body. The question of access to housing versus access to territory is a very sticky one, indeed, but could have far-reaching implications for the pattern of distribution of black households within metropolitan systems.

The ghetto appears to be a fixed feature of urban real estate in American cities in that its disappearance is nowhere in sight. No amount of physical tampering with these configurations has reduced the extent of their territorial base. Attempts to modify the ghettos as physical entities, especially efforts, designed to break them up, have met with failure, for the physical entity itself is simply an expression of a set of forces which allocate housing to black people in such a manner as to give rise to such physical entities. Thus, the removal of a segment of that entity, through urban renewal or any of the other programs engaged in urban redevelopment, only leads to the regeneration of additional appendages contiguous to the main body of the entity, since the basic ghetto forming process is left unaltered.

THE ROLE OF BLACK PERCEPTION

The central issue here is, How does one move beyond this point? The question is not one of whether black territorial communities should exist, but under what conditions they should exist. Their present existence is based on an absence of locational options, which tends to exert a strong influence on where they will be sited within a metropolitan system. So long as community locational determinations are constrained in this manner, then the ghetto label is not inappropriate. One can imagine the holding of a plebiscite with black people being asked to vote on the question of whether they would prefer to leave or stay within a zone now locally referred to as the ghetto, and the outcome being used to determine the community's identity. If the majority of the people chose to reside within the zone of the current residence, then the ghetto designation would no longer be appropriate. Better still, if the majority of these persons surveyed chose to reside in an alternative environment in which most of their neighbors were black, then the use of the term ghetto to describe this new residential environment would likewise be inappropriate. When freedom of choice is allowed to prevail, then and only then will black people be able to identify their own communities. But it is likewise then and only then that such externally imposed identities will become meaningless.

The point to be made here is that black residential communities, of whatever level of intensity of black occupancy or whatever condition of physical repair, need not be identified as ghettos if the residents are given a choice of access. Thus, it is possible for those places that have been described throughout this book to conceptually diasppear tomorrow simply as a result of people indicating that the current zone of residential occupancy represents their preference. But the prospects for this are highly unlikely, and the problems that permeate those communities would still be with us.

STRATEGIES FOR CHANGE

The problematic aspects associated with the development of black territorial based communities have prompted public officials and private organizations alike to investigate the feasibility of developing alternative residential patterns. To date, few workable alternatives have been experimented with. This is the likely result of national internal conflict stemming from a philosophical commitment to racial integration and the private practice of racial exclusiveness. This conflict is further complicated by the emphasis on individual freedom in the society at large and the substitution of the group for the individual in the black subpopulation. In terms of action, it appears that as long as most blacks are considered to hold membership in an underclass, their rights as individuals will receive only limited attention. Of course, the conditions which are responsible for most blacks being viewed as members of an underclass have made it necessary for the group to seek relief from this situation via the class action route. Thus the black man's historical lot in this country has made it necessary to minimize the role of the individual as a means of altering the lot of the group. And this in turn continues to complicate the dilemma.

Blacks themselves are fully aware of this problem as expressions of black unity tend to substantiate the notion of oneness. Such expressions as, "No black man is free until all black people are free," tend to sum up the feeling that efforts to alter the lot of the group require a oneness of action. On the other hand, when serious disagreements exist among segments of the black community—the white population will note that it is ironic that they cannot agree among themselves—it is an indication of black support of the oneness of the individual with the group. White officials often choose to recognize the views of only those black subgroups which are compatible with theirs as representing the legitimate expression of black community concern.

Alternative Racial Residential Patterns

During the period of the late sixties when urban violence was at a peak, public attention began to shift to the conditions in the ghetto and possibilities for change. Downs, during his association with the

Kerner Commission of this era, posited a set of alternative strategies designed to alter the nature of the ghetto configuration. The Downs' alternatives have been described as follows:[3] (1) concentration, segregation, nonenrichment; (2) concentration, segregation, enrichment; (3) concentration, integration, enrichment (the integrated core strategy); (4) dispersal, segregation, enrichment; and (5) dispersal, integration, enrichment. In considering this set of alternative strategies, number one can be eliminated for it is the noninterventionist strategy. Strategy number two appears to be the one currently receiving the greatest Federal support in terms of programming efforts. The model cities program can be considered a tactic designed to lend support to this strategy. The concept of "new towns in town" likewise would be supportive of strategy two. Strategy three is represented by current attempts to promote low-income housing on scattered sites. Only a few cities have approved these latter efforts as a compromise measure after much behind-the-scenes discussion. To date, scattered sites developments are generally still in the planning stage.

The dispersal strategies suggested by Downs are beginning to bring blacks into suburbia. Preliminary evidence suggests that black suburbanization is basically associated with strategy four, which is the dispersal, segregation strategy. Thus, while most of the suggested strategies are designed to improve the residential environment, those which are currently operative tend to leave territorial segregation intact. Strategy two is slowly beginning to provide extra amenities within inner-city environments but on a very limited scale, while strategy four increases black suburbanization and thereby presents blacks with a greater variety of environmental options. But often these two strategies are indistinguishable, as black suburbanization in many instances simply represents spillover beyond the boundaries of the central city. In those instances where individual black residential clusters have evolved within a suburban setting far removed from the location of central-city ghettos, then the two strategies can be identified as being mutually exclusive.

Alternative Strategies and the Role of Income

Because blacks continue to be found disproportionately along the lower rung of the income ladder in this country, governmental assistance will be required to activate all but one of the previously mentioned strategies. During the latter half of the sixties a number of Federally supported housing programs were designed to place suitable housing within easy access of that segment of the population

[3] *Ibid.*, p. 1345.

that would normally encounter difficulty because of income limitations.

A variety of Federal housing subsidies have aided in transforming the nation from a nation of renters to a nation of owners. In 1930 roughly one-third of the nation's households were owner-occupied, but by 1960 the incidence had reached two-thirds, one-half of which were able to move into this category as a result of the FHA and VA mortgage guarantee programs.[4] Until recently all Federally subsidized housing programs designed to provide shelter for the poor concentrated on increasing the supply of rental housing. Thus, blacks who had failed to share proportionately in previous governmental efforts designed to make owners out of renters were now able to participate in programs in which home ownership was not the principal goal. Outside of public housing, black access to Federally subsidized housing on any meaningful scale did not occur until the adoption of the 221(d)(3) program in 1961.

The 221(d)(3) program was designed to make rental housing available to persons of moderate income, and not until the adoption of the 221(h) program was free standing owner-occupancy housing made available to purchasers at below mortgage interest rates. During the early sixties Weaver indicated that the 221(d)(3) program was making a new kind of housing package available to blacks in the South,[5] and likewise indicated that it might be expected to produce biracial housing accommodations in selected locations outside the South.[6] Thus there is some evidence that the Federal housing programs of the early sixties possibly made a minimal contribution to the enrichment strategy described previously, but the number of units financed under the 221 program was a very small fraction of the number of single family for-sale units guaranteed by FHA over the same period of time. The successor program to 221(d)(3) and 221(h) are the 236 and 235 programs which came out of the housing act of 1968.

Unlike their predecessors, the latter programs were designed to provide new housing for low-income families rather than moderate-income families. There are some who question the contention that this housing is in fact being produced for low-income families. Taggart indicates that this program has been more successful in dispersing low-income housing outside the blighted inner-city areas than has any previous subsidy program, but agrees that since there is

[4] Frank S. Sengstock and Mary C. Sengstock, "Homeownership: A Goal for All Americans," *Journal of Urban Law,* Vol. 46, Issue 3, 1969, p. 160.

[5] Robert D. Weaver, *The Urban Complex,* Doubleday & Co., Inc., Garden City, N.Y., 1964, p. 253.

[6] *Ibid.,* p. 254.

no data available on the racial mix of the housing that "the impression is that its success is due in large part to 'creaming' of the clientele it serves, for instance, by choice of 'low-income' families whose head is in college."[7] The 235 program, just as was true of 221(d)(3), has probably been more effective in making housing available to blacks in noncentral city areas in the South than it has in the North for reasons previously discussed.

There is much opposition from suburban communities in general to the development of 235 housing within their boundaries, as it is contended that it would lower existing housing values and overcrowd the schools. Thus, the one mechanism which it was thought might possibly foster dispersal of blacks beyond the margins of the central city does not appear to be the appropriate vehicle. The weakness of the vehicle for this purpose is partially associated with the scale of development of housing within this program. Often developers are able to put together a large parcel whereupon a number of units are built under the program, thereby creating an image of public housing, even though these are free-standing for-sale-to-owner units.

It is likely that blacks would encounter less opposition if they were permitted to purchase individual units outside of the context of tract developments. This is now possible under the section of the program dealing with purchase of older rehabilitated homes, which accounts for a small share of the total housing that might be purchased within the limitations of the program. It is quite possible that blacks have benefited most from this segment of the program. The present practice of housing development under 235 is likely to benefit the building construction industry to a much greater extent than it will benefit low-income black families, unless there are available sites for construction present within the existing ghetto configuration.

A FINAL COMMENT

Of the various strategies outlined by Downs, all are likely to be observed operating at various levels in individual places throughout the nation. Given the existing historical base, that is what might be expected. But it is critical that those strategies which are most promising in changing the lot of the black population in America should be given the greatest support. The combination of low income among the black population, life styles which permit one to cope with his local environment but at the same time create obstacles which make it difficult to penetrate the larger environment, and ultimately simple prejudice, would justify one's hedging his bets on

[7] Robert Taggart III, *Low-Income Housing: A Critique of Federal Aid,* The Johns Hopkins University Press, Baltimore, Md., 1971, p. 79.

strategies one and two, for they require little more than is currently being done. Strategies four and five are likely to meet with opposition from whites who perceive blacks as a threat in either an economic, social, or psychological sense, or some combination of them all, and from some blacks who view the evolution of a political power base if strategies one and two are allowed continued domination. In the final analysis, the strategy which is likely to dominate will reflect a complex combination of black and white response to changes in economic conditions and social environments.

It would be possible to dismiss the whole issue on this note if other forces in urban America could be held constant, while blacks and whites resolved whatever differences serve as the basis for the present dilemma. But since this is not the case, it is necessary to intervene in such a way as to create a diversity of satisfactory residential environments that will provide an appropriate combination of economic, social, psychic, and cultural resources to satisfy the needs of a diverse black population. In some instances this will mean emphasizing strategy two, while in others it will mean emphasizing strategies four and five. So both "new towns in towns" and "new towns" possess some merit in arriving at the kind of residential environment that will provide black Americans with a choice of where they shall live.

In the past the new-towns-in-towns concept has essentially represented rhetoric designed to make residential segregation more palatable, while the new-towns concept has represented intellectual idealism. Although recently Alonzo indicated that some planners viewed new towns as places where migrants destined for the cities could be acculturated,[8] yet the whole notion of black culture and a satisfactory living environment remains incompletely explored, and thus the relationship between the two is not well understood.

Whatever the nature and spatial residential patterns of future black urban populations, they should evolve out of freedom of choice, made as a result of rational decisions designed to provide each individual and family with access to the kind of support system that promotes healthy growth and a stable social system. The present geography of urban black populations is simply a reflection of the way the existing social system functions. It is possible for the system to function differently and the same patterns to remain intact, but this is highly unlikely. Residential systems which evolve out of freedom of choice promote the development of communities of interest regardless of racial makeup. If and when blacks in America are provided with this option, the black ghetto will disappear and

[8] William Alonzo, "What Are New Towns For?," *Urban Studies,* Feb., 1970, p. 14.

will be replaced by social communities based on commonality of interest, which might in fact range from 100 percent black to 1 percent black. If and when this occurs, the ghetto will be an inappropriate lable to describe communities found anywhere along this spectrum.